Life for a Wanderer

ANDREW M. GREELEY

Life for a Wanderer

DOUBLEDAY & COMPANY, INC., GARDEN CITY, NEW YORK
1969

248.4
Cot

Contents

These all died in faith, not having received what was promised but having seen it from afar and having acknowledged that they were strangers and wanderers on earth. For people who speak thus make it clear that they are seeking a homeland . . . they desire a better country. Heb. 11:13–16

For the Salettas   Jack and Suzie,
whom I met on the "courts" so long ago.
Or was it only yesterday?

Introduction

One should begin a book, and particularly a book on the spiritual life, with some sort of explanation as to why one has chosen to write it that goes beyond the simple confession that my good friend Dan Herr, president of that outstanding purveyor of Catholic literature, the Thomas More Association, has told me to write it.

Since the early days of Christianity, followers of Jesus of Nazareth have tried to set down on paper their interpretations of what the gospel implies for human living. The tradition of asceticism which has resulted from some of these efforts is a broad one consuming such diverse viewpoints as that of the penitential "fathers of the deserts" as well as the nobleman's guide to sanctity provided by Francis de Sales. Like all things ancient, the Christian spiritual tradition has been faced with the peril of becoming traditionalist, although such works as the *Imitation of Christ, Introduction to the Devout Life,* and *The Spiritual Exercises* possess the vitality and the wisdom which enable them to transcend partially the cultural barriers imposed by the era which produced them. But, as the tradition has come down to many of us, it has frequently seemed dry, stagnant, and juridic; hence, in the great sweep of energies

unleashed by the Vatican Council, there has been a tendency
to reject the spiritual tradition as obsolete in an age of psy-
choanalysis and personalism.

In one sociological study, for example, a respondent who
would admit to having read the books of Father Edward Leen,
had a point scored against her as a conservative. Leaving aside
the dubious sociology of such a judgment, one is still forced
to conclude that the tradition of which Leen is by no means
the least able exponent, has come upon hard times.

Yet there are many of us who were raised in this spiritual
tradition and who have no doubt about its inadequacy in the
form it was presented to us who, nonetheless, are not altogether
sure that it ought to be rejected completely. The human person
was not discovered by Kierkegaard, nor was the human unconscious discovered by Sigmund Freud, even though these two
geniuses made tremendous contributions to our understanding
of personality and the unconscious. The wisdom out of the
past may be inadequate and incomplete, but that is not to
say that it is worthless or that we have nothing to learn from
it.

Thus it is not necessary, nor even very wise, for the present
generation to assume that it must begin anew and develop a
new and totally modern Christian spirituality. A much better
case can be made for the argument that the vital element
within the Christian condition not only admits of updating, but
demands it. In my own personal life, I must say that my
work in the behavioral sciences, far from leading me to reject
this vital core of the ascetical tradition, has helped me to
understand it for the first time.

I do not propose to attempt in this volume a summary of
the principal points of the tradition of Christian spirituality, nor
will I point out where and how it can be updated in the
light of the behavioral sciences. A strong case could be made
for such a volume, but I am not sure that I am the one to
write it, and, in any event, I do not at the present time want
to write it.

What I much prefer to do (and what Mr. Herr has told me to do) is to present a series of reflections on what the Christian life seems to me to mean in the contemporary world. In the process of doing this, I shall make suggestions as to how some of the traditional concepts of the Christian spirituality—faith, hope, charity, poverty, chastity, obedience, justice, temperance, fortitude, prudence—might be interpreted in the lives of contemporary man. I do not want to assert that my interpretation is the only possible one, nor that my description of, let us say, justice is necessarily consistent with what has been said about justice in the past. All I care to say is that my vision of the Christian life, seen as it may be through the perspective of a social scientist, is still profoundly shaped by the wisdom of years gone by, a wisdom which was passed on to me, however imperfectly, by those who attempted to train me in that tradition.

More vigorous claims than this I will not make. The book is obviously one man's view of what is the Christian life's meaning and practice. If such a view is useful to others, either intellectually or practically, then so much the better. If it is not, then I am sure that the Thomas More Association will peddle most of the excess copies at its annual Fabulous February bargain sale.

I have titled the volume *Life for a Wanderer* because it has often seemed to me in recent years that the Christian life is a form of wandering. The Christian has in both ancient and contemporary writing frequently been described as a traveler or a pilgrim. I have no particular quarrel with this image, but in the modern world traveling and pilgrimage may mean something less than they did in the past. Much of the uncertainty, the ambiguity, and the danger has been removed from travel. From my office in Chicago I am but two hours from almost any city in the United States, save those on the West Coast, and less than two days from any place in the world. The only high adventure facing me is the ride on the Chicago expressway system to O'Hare International Airport and the only

uncertainty is whether the landing and the take-off delays at
O'Hare will be half an hour or more than half an hour.

The term "wandering" therefore conveys to me something
of the experimental and exploratory nature of the Christian
life, the "playing it by ear" which traveling and pilgrimage
do not convey. The Christian knows, vaguely at least, where
he is going, but he is not quite sure how, specifically, he is
going to get there. Hence he is forced to be experimental, to
try one path for a while and then to leave it if it does not
seem to be headed for his destination; to follow one set of
charts for a time, but to be prepared always to cast these
charts aside when a better set is offered him. To change the
image somewhat, he is like a sailor who adjusts the sails on
his ship with the changing directions of the wind, since he
knows as every good sailor does that the wind is inclined to
blow whither it will.

There may well be more of the wandering element in Christian life at some times than at others, but surely in the Era
of Uncertainty which has emerged from the Vatican Council,
the wandering element is a strong one. My own life has shaped
not only the viewpoint I am expressing in this volume, but
also the very notion of the Christian life as wandering.*

I will not argue that my peregrinations around the nation and
the world as an itinerant sociologist earn me the title of
"wanderer," but I do feel that I am very much the marginal
man, living on the fringes between the Church and the secular
university and being viewed by both as something of a deviant
(too secular for the Catholics and too Catholic for the seculars,
as my colleague Peter Rossi has put it). This marginality presents
what a Christian life ought to be. For we who are followers of
Jesus of Nazareth must necessarily stand on the margins of our
society, very much part of the society and yet representing
something transcendent. Only if we're willing to stand on the

---

* Warren Bennis of State University of New York at Buffalo has argued
that I am one of the few academicians he knows whose life is evidence
against the theory of his ingenious volume *The Temporary Society*.

margins can we "hang loose," "travel light," and "play it by ear." It is in these directions that the Lord pointed us when he said that he did not even have a place whereon to lay his head. Most of us have pretty comfortable beds, yet like Daniel Boone we must always live in such a way that we are ready to "move out" when irresistible opportunity presents itself. Like Boone, we who are Christians should be the avant-garde, the scouts, the pioneers, the explorers. Somewhere out there where man has not yet traveled is the way we must go as we blaze the trail which others will follow behind us. We have come a long way and yet there is still a long way to go, but, unlike John Wayne and the other western heroes riding off into the sunset, the light we are wandering toward is the sunrise.

1. *It's Out There Somewhere* (FAITH)

Some time ago a young man approached me with considerable anxiety about the fact that he was "losing his faith." The problem seemed to be that he had trouble believing in guardian angels, indeed angels of any kind, and didn't see how he could remain a Catholic in good faith if he found it necessary to reject the teaching of the Church about guardian angels.

I really don't think that this was the young man's problem. On the contrary, I suspect his problems were far more psychological than intellectual, but it was still with considerable difficulty that I restrained my laughter; for the thought of someone rejecting Christianity on the issue of guardian angels does seem just a bit ludicrous. There are many doctrines which are harder to swallow than that, like the Trinity, for example.

But the young man's problem, at least insofar as it was an intellectual problem, resulted from the fact that he had been trained to believe that faith is essentially an assent to a series of propositions, a series which periodically grows longer as new propositions are added by one kind of authority or another. He was taught that the system of propositions is so linked that if one rejects one of them, the system comes tumbling down upon him. If you do not, for example, believe that there is a guardian angel hovering next to you, then the edifice of Catholic Christianity has collapsed for you.

Others somewhat more sophisticated than this young man perceive a certain hierarchy in the catalogue of propositions which "must be believed under pain of mortal sin," and near the top of the list of course, if not at the very top, is a doctrine of papal infallibility. It is basically useless to attempt to deal with someone whose "objections" against "the Faith" rest on difficulties about papal infallibility. Clearly, a church needs some kind of leadership and clearly too, some kind of special charisma must be attached to that leadership, but it is also obvious to anyone who reads the history books, or even the newspapers, that a great many mistakes and a great deal of incompetency coexists with the special charisma that the leadership of the Church enjoys. It is not my intention to deny papal infallibility or to deny guardian angels or to deny a need for propositional orthodoxy or indeed to deny anything. In this volume, I simply want to argue that faith is more than a series of propositional affirmations and far more than one's acceptance of the charisma of the chief bishop of the Catholic Church. That issue is not an unimportant one, but it is not one where the critical difference between faith and unbelief is to be found, nor one, I think, where a great deal of time can be strategically utilized in discussion.

Faith may involve propositional assent but it is far more than that. It is, rather, a basic and integrated orientation of the total personality, an orientation which in the Catholic tradition shapes the style and the posture of man's relationship to God, to Christ, to the world, to life and death, and to his fellowman. Such a basic orientation reaches to the very roots of a human personality and gives color and tone and shape to all the behavior in which a man engages. To think that this orientation can be "lost" because one is not sure whether God's providence is exercised over us through disembodied spirits or whether the Roman pontiff may be wrong on certain matters of doctrine seems to me to be hopelessly naïve. Intellectual problems can create an imbalance in a basic and pervasive personality orientation, an imbalance which is both disquieting and uncomfortable, but they cannot, I think, destroy such an orientation of the personality unless it is already very weak.

Faith is, first of all, an orientation toward God. It is not based on our confidence that we can give a completely convincing rational proof for the existence of God. Faith is rather a commitment to goodness, a deep conviction that the world, human life, and one's own life have meaning, purpose, dignity, and beauty—a commitment which cannot be made unless one is willing to admit that there is Something in life which transcends life. A "belief" in God is in fact a refusal to concede that human existence is purposeless, ugly, and evil. While this commitment to goodness may seem very sketchy, and while in the Christian tradition it is enriched and developed by several other commitments, it is nonetheless the most difficult of all to make. The empirical data against it are powerful. Life does appear mean, ugly, and vicious on many occasions and one must make a mighty leap of faith to commit oneself to graciousness despite the data to the contrary. (It must be remarked that a leap of faith is required to reject graciousness as well as to accept it and that the posture of refusing to decide for or against graciousness may be intellectually respectable, but is probably emotionally impossible.)

The second commitment that a Christian makes is to Christ, in whom God has revealed himself to men in a very special way, a way which occurred but once in human experience. To state it this way is by no means to reject the formulae of the Council of Chalcedon; but it is merely to point out that men made their commitment to the specialness of the theophany in Christ, for several centuries before Chalcedon, without having its neat formulae available; as time goes on one can suppose that believers will find other formulae which are even more accurate and precise representations of their commitment to Christ than those provided by Chalcedon. Christ is someone

special, for God is in him in a special way and we are committed
to that at a much deeper level of our personality than any
propositional statements can adequately represent. Christ is
unique, Christ is *the* representative of God, *the model* to our
lives, *the* prophet of our vision, *the* assurance of goodness,
the way, *the* truth, *the* life.* Not only do we view Christ as a
theophany, we view him as a redeeming and life-bringing theophany. With the life of Jesus, something new and dramatically
different was introduced into the human experience. A promise
was made, a promise that sin and death were being conquered
and that man would rise. The theophany which is Christ is an
Easter theophany, a theophany which is a promise of resurrection.
In our orientation toward God, we Christians commit ourselves to
a belief in goodness. In our orientation toward Christ, we commit
ourselves to a belief that goodness is so extensive and so powerful
that it triumphs even over death. From the viewpoint of history
it is easy for us to see that the two are ultimately inseparable,
that one cannot be committed to goodness without necessarily
hoping for resurrection. As Brian Wicker *Toward a Contemporary Christianity* puts it, the Christian is merely the humanist
who is sure of the ground on which he stands. Nonetheless,
most men did not have the courage to push their commitment to
goodness to include a commitment to resurrection until the
theophany of Jesus forced men to make a choice either for
or against resurrection. "If Christ be not risen from the dead,
our faith is in vain."

From this commitment to the promise of resurrection there
follows an orientation toward the world. The Christian views
the world not as evil but as less than perfect. It is, although

* To keep the heresy hunters at bay, let me also assert that I accept completely and totally the notion that He is the Son of God, the second
person of the Blessed Trinity. And while I'm at it, let me assert also that I
affirm every other proposition of the Catholic faith and ask the heresy
hunters to put aside their magnifying glasses. What I am attempting to do
in this volume is to state the implications of this faith for our personal lives
in a language which is different from that of the technical theological
language.

he would only have used the word recently, an evolutionary world, a world that is moving toward resurrection, a world on a pilgrimage, a wandering world. Since man is destined for resurrection, his body is sacred; and since his body is part of the world, then the world too is sacred. As St. Paul says it, the world together with man is groaning toward redemption.

The Christian is under no illusions about the world; he knows that it is imperfect and at times a dangerous place, he may even occasionally withdraw from it; but he also realizes that it is physically and psychologically impossible, and indeed immoral for him to be alienated from it. It is not only the site of his pilgrimage, it is also a fellow pilgrim. Even if it is not perfect, it is still good, and the good things in it, both natural and man-made, are of God. While the Christian must use these good things gently, he still uses them joyously. He knows temptation to compulsiveness about the world but he also understands that his commitment to the Promise is a commitment to the eventual elimination of compulsiveness.

The Christian also has a certain orientation toward life and toward death. He loves life and fears death, but he believes that death is an illusion—a painful, terrifying, mysterious illusion, but an illusion nonetheless. He knows he cannot escape it, he lives in preparation for it, but he also understands that morbidity is a poor preparation for death. Seizing the opportunities of life is the only adequate response that someone who has made a commitment to the resurrection promise can maintain in the face of the mystery of death. Death is the payoff question. One can make commitments to goodness and to the theophany of Christ and even to an evolutionary world without having to face the question of one's own personal destiny. But to assert that death is an illusion forces one to reexamine once again the authenticity and the sincerity of one's overarching commitment to goodness.

Finally, the Christian has an orientation toward his fellowmen. He does not agree with Jean Paul Sartre that hell is other people, though on occasion, at least, he may suspect that purgatory is other people. The Christian believes that mankind is one, that the Church is a continuation of Christ's mission of reuniting the fractured segments of mankind, that the Church is the bearer of good news of the resurrection promise, that about this good news it cannot be wrong. He knows the Church is inadequate, incomplete, and growing. He knows that fear and distrust abound in the Church, and thus inhibit the free flow of love which is the only way that mankind can become one once again. He also realizes that love between and among members of the Church is the primary technique that Jesus left to his followers for preaching the good news of the resurrection promise; "By this shall all men know that you are my disciples, that you have love for one another." So his commitment to the Church is a commitment to all mankind and a commitment to love and to trust, a commitment which is terribly difficult to practice, but one about which the Christian knows there is no choice.

These are the critical issues of the Christian faith, issues of God, Christ, world, life and death, and fellowman. They are issues which, while they surely include cognitive propositions, also transcend these propositions. They are also, for all practical purposes, one package, a package the acceptance of which requires a leap of faith. The teaching of the Church and the speculating of its theologians are merely attempts, sometimes quite successful and sometimes less so, to clarify and explicate the implications of this "package" of faith. If all the focus in our thinking is on questions which are peripheral to these critical issues, then the clarification which is the role of teachers is less than successful. If we think, for example, that Christianity has to do essentially with papacy or hierarchy or the Assumption, to the exclusion of the basic good news and the basic leap of faith involved in commitment to the good news, then we have badly missed the point. If, on the other hand, we can accept the basic commitment to the good news and have problems about more peripheral propositions, it is difficult to see why these problems need to be immediately resolved. There is little ambiguity in many catechisms, but there is much ambiguity in human life and only the immature and the malcontent are frustrated by ambiguity. I'm not arguing against attempts at clarifying aspects of Christianity which continue to trouble us, I'm just arguing that most of the problems which seem to trouble most people frequently appear to be pretexts for avoiding the awesome and indeed cataclysmic questions involved in the basic issues.

What are we to say when someone informs us that he does not believe in "confession"? Does he mean that he does not have to go to confession frequently? Well and good—no one said he did. Does he mean that sins can be forgiven in other ways besides telling them to a priest? Again, this is a position for which there is almost unanimous support in the theological manuals. Does he mean that he feels he does not have to go to confession before going to communion? Such an assertion merely brings him in line with the traditional teaching of the manuals. But is he trying to say that he does not believe in sin or in the forgiveness of sin, or that Jesus came to undo the effects of sin, or that his Church does not continue that curative work? Then we are forced to say that he is touching on questions which are relevant to the basic issues, for if he denies moral evil, or if he denies the power to cure moral evil, then he is either rejecting the need for good news, or its effectiveness.

Or finally, he is telling us that he does not believe the curative power can be exercised in a tête-à-tête or that he doesn't believe in the way the sacrament of penance was taught or administered in his youth, or that he does not believe there is a psychological advantage in auricular confession. If these are his problems, we must reply that psychological evidence for spiritual healing in tête-à-têtes is overwhelming, indeed so overwhelming that in the Church for countless centuries there was the practice of confessing one's sins to other lay people (a practice which theologians have been inclined in more recent years to write off as non-sacramental—though there is no evidence that the people engaged in it thought it was non-sacramental). If his objection is to the way it was taught to him in grammar school and administered to him on the Thursday before First Friday, then he has every reason to object; but this doesn't mean that he does not believe in sin or the forgiveness of sins or in the promise of a resurrection when sin and evil will be ultimately conquered.

When we focus on one issue and torment ourselves with worry over that issue, we have completely obscured the meaning of Christianity. We are saying there is one tree in the forest that disturbs us and that therefore it is necessary to chop down all the trees in the forest—which forest we have not been able to investigate because we are so fixated on the single unpleasant tree. If we wish to see all the scattered propositions which constitute the "deposit of faith" with some sort of integrated unity, then we must try to see them in their relationship to the basic issues of God, Christ, the world, life, death, fellowmen. To isolate the specific propositions from the basic issues is to cut the branches off the vine.

It is a long, long way, for example, from the good news of the gospels to the bad news of *Humanae Vitae* and the unclear theory of "religious assent" which is invoked to demand compliance to that highly controversial encyclical. The connection between such assent and the basic issues is a thin one. I'm not saying that the connection is invalid, but the commitment to the Christian solution to the basic issues can hardly, in any intelligent sense of the words, be said to rest on our reaction to an encyclical or our notion of what sort of assent is appropriate to the ordinary teaching of the head of the Church. Let me stress once again that I do not mean that these latter questions are unimportant, but I do insist that they differ qualitatively from the basic issues.

I would be the last one, for example, to say that the papacy is an unimportant question, but I also fail to see how we can permit it to become the most important question that we as Christians face. The Christian community to which we have committed ourselves as part of our response to the basic issues does require a religious leader, a religious leader who has special powers and deserves special reverence, and whose position merits special explanation.

All religious leaders, of course, are seen as having special powers and the mode of acknowledging these powers differs from Paul VI to Eugene Carson Blake to Arthur Michael Ramsey. If one wishes to ask, apart from theorizing, which one of these three men has the most *effective* influence among his followers at the present time, one might have to give the vote to Ramsey —which points out that all the theories in the world are no substitute for intelligent and dynamic leadership.

The First Vatican Council was a way of explaining the special nature of the papal leadership, a way of saying it was especially special. That Council's description of the nature of papal leadership must be seen as an organic development of the tradition about such leadership, but not by any means the completion of a tradition, nor the end of its development.

The real problem is that the controversy over this Vatican Council and the interpretation that some try to put on its decisions led many of us to believe, at least in some level of our personalities, that the Church existed for the papacy instead of the papacy for the Church and for the good news which the Church conveys. The root of the problem was that we permitted a specific and very important issue to be separated from the basic issues. It is precisely the isolation of peripheral questions from the basic issues which makes them problems, an isolation which generally takes place when simplifiers and popularizers simplify and popularize so much that the good news vanishes from the presentation of the faith. If we see the Pope as the absolutely necessary and inevitable leader the Christian community must have, then we see the issue of the papacy where it belongs, as a question intimately and closely related to the basic issues, but one which does not by itself substitute for the basic issues. If in our own thinking we permit such a substitution to take place, then we will miss the whole point of the Christian faith.

The Christian as a man of faith is not someone necessarily who can recite and explain the creeds with all the nuance of theological sophistication. There were many men of faith before there were creeds and very many men of faith before there were sophisticated theological explanations. The man of faith is one who holds determinedly to the commitment of the Christian response to the basic issues, *no matter what happens*. The problem with many who have "lost" their faith is that they never understood the basic issues, never accepted the Christian response to them; or in times of emotional and intellectual confusion they lost sight of the basic issues and lost insight into the Christian response. As one theologian put it to me, a good Christian doesn't really believe very much, but what he believes he believes unshakably. If one may adjust words just a bit and say that we *believe* our response to the basic issues and *accept* the doctrinal propositions which cluster around these issues, then this theologian's statement seems to be unarguable. But if our time, our energies, and our concerns are focused far more on the things we accept than on the things we really believe, there is a dangerous imbalance in our faith.

The Christian faith is an interpretive scheme which copes with the ultimate questions man must ask himself, questions to which there are no demonstrable answers—at least demonstrable in the sense that modern science uses the word. It is to these issues that every man must address himself. If he flees to lose himself in peripheral questions, he's either blind or a coward.

Perhaps there is but one basic issue and that is the issue of goodness, death, resurrection—either we believe in resurrection and commit our whole life to it or we do not. Either we dismiss the good news as too good to be true, or we permit ourselves to be overwhelmed by its joyfulness and then become overwhelmingly joyful persons because of it. We who are Christians ought to have done with undue wrangling over the wording of propositions* and devote our energies to rejoicing in such a way that our joy becomes a light that shines among men. One wonders how many have been converted to accepting the possibility of the good news by all the heresy trials, by all the condemnations, by all the inquisitions and investigations, by all the anguish over preserving the deposit of faith from being tainted that the history of Christendom has produced.

Is the "deposit of faith," after all, that weak, is Christ's good news that obscure, is our faith that lifeless, is the resurrection promise that easily misinterpreted that we devote so much of our time and energy to preserving it from mistake or corruption? I am not saying that we should abandon all care over issues of orthodoxy; there are interpretations of the good news which make it either not good or not news. Nor do I want to take the anti-intellectual position that ideas and the categories that convey them are unimportant. I simply want to assert, as I have throughout this chapter, that they are not all-important and that if they substitute for joyous commitment to the good news of the Christian response to the basic issues, then something profoundly wrong has happened.

The man of faith, then, believes, and believes strongly; he believes and he believes joyously; he believes and he believes wisely; he doesn't have all the answers; he doesn't know how every problem is to be solved. He knows that there is much more to be discovered. He is open-minded about the pursuit of answers to the as yet unanswered questions. He is still a wanderer and he realizes that he is wandering in a fog, but he knows where he is going, even if he is not sure how he is going to get there. He knows that he *will* get there and he even has some idea of what it will be like. You can get

---

* Which is not to say the wording of propositions is unimportant but merely to say that it is not as important as our joy over and our commitment to our resurrection promise.

into an argument with him but you can't shake him; you can puzzle him but you cannot confuse him; you can worry him but you cannot take away his joy; you'd better beware of him, for the joy that the insights of his interpretive scheme bring to him is contagious. You might catch it if you don't watch out.

2. *They Can't Mean Me*
(LOVE)

Luis Buñuel's movie *Belle de Jour* is an extraordinarily insightful, sensitive presentation of the great spiritual problems of self-hatred. Severine, it's heroine, filled with guilt and self-loathing because of a sin (apparently incest) in the past, is unable to respond to her husband's love. The only sort of sex which can have any meaning for her is that in which she is punished and degraded. She takes on a "part-time job" in a discreet Paris brothel, and becomes involved with a vicious and half-mad young criminal who shoots her husband in a fit of jealousy and is himself killed by the police. A friend tells the paralyzed husband about the heroine's secret life; he forgives her and loves her even in this abyss of degradation in which she has put herself. Seeing that she is loved, no matter how much evil she has done, Severine begins the long climb back to self-respect and self-esteem.*

* Almost everyone who sees the movie has his own interpretation of the enigmatic ending, apparently even the actors themselves weren't quite sure what to make of it. My own inclination is to think that the psychological dynamics which Buñuel so carefully probes are such that the fantasy at the end is that her husband is still paralyzed and the reality is that he is not. Severine still indulges in fantasies of self-punishment, but the fantasies are minor and fleeting.

The theme of *Belle de Jour* is an ancient one in the Judeo-Christian tradition, clearly very reminiscent of the story of the prophet Hosea. The secret of Buñuel's triumph is that aided by the insights of modern psychology, he's able to see the Hosea myth from the point of view of the faithless wife and understand the psychodynamics behind such faithlessness. The insight of *Belle de Jour* becomes extremely important for the Christian life if we realize that the faithless wife represents in the Judeo-Christian tradition both God's people and the individual believer. Severine was faithless because she hated herself, so God's people are faithless because they do not value themselves and the individual believer is faithless because he does not have enough self-esteem. Contrary to older interpretations, pride and it's allies hatred, envy, and anger are rooted not in too much self-esteem but rather in the lack of self-esteem. The proud person doesn't love himself too much; rather, he loves himself not enough.

Modern psychology also enables us to see another implication of the Hosea myth: Hosea's faithless wife, Magdalene, and the Church as bride are not evil; the love of the faithful lover does not turn evil into good. Severine's husband does not love her because she is evil, he loves her for the reasons any man loves his wife, because she is good and lovable. He sees the good that she does not see in herself and by affirming this good in the face of powerful evidence to the contrary, he enables the good to grow and to conquer fear and hatred. So God's love is not a love which covers up evil. Rather, it acknowledges the good in his people and acknowledges it so repeatedly and so insistently that the faithless spouse must eventually respond in agreement. God's mission in the world and his mission in his relationship with the individual believer is essentially a mission of overcoming self-hatred. For self-hatred is a barrier to love. We hate other people not because we love ourselves too much but because we are not able to love ourselves enough. We fear and distrust them because we feel inadequate in our relationships to them, we hide behind hatred and anger because in some deep

recess of our personality we do not think we are good enough
for them.

The Hosea myth, repeated as it is so often in the Old and New
Testaments, reinforces the profound psychological insight of
the dictum that we should love our neighbor as ourselves; for if
we do not love ourselves, we are not able to love our neighbor.
On the contrary, our self-hatred will force us to hate him because we fear and distrust him. As strong as this insight is in
the Christian tradition, it has not prevented rampant self-hatred
from masquerading as virtue and sometimes almost dominating
the themes of Christian spirituality. Presumably our psychological insights are sophisticated enough today that we will never
have a saint again who, despite the immense consciousness of
his own dignity which must have been necessary for him to be
a saint, would still feel constrained to proclaim constantly that
he was a worm and no man. We are not worms. We are men
with faults, and failings and weaknesses, but also men who are
worth far more than we ever dare to admit to ourselves.

In the previous chapter we argued that faith involved basic
orientations and basic commitments toward God, Christ, the
world, life, death and our fellowmen, but there is another basic
commitment that is essential, and that is the commitment to ourselves, a belief in our own worth and dignity and value. We
may in theory distinguish between faith and love but in fact
faith in oneself and love for oneself are quite indistinguish-
able. If we do not have this quality (which could also be called
by the somewhat less traditional name of self-esteem), then the
other commitments in our life, be they to God's goodness or to
the goodness of those around us, will be severely impaired.
Only he who accepts himself and believes in himself is free to
commit himself to the goodness around him.

This is a basic area of convergence between Freudianism and
Christianity: both believe in the dignity of the individual person.
Both believe that the good is the real self and that the evil
which, in St. Paul's words, we would not do is the hate that we
feel for ourselves. Original sin, at least on the phenomenological

level, is the fact that we do not receive enough love in our
early years to have an adequate self-evaluation or the ability to
give ourselves fully in love to others. The circle of good or the
circle of evil in which we become involved is merely a reflection
of the balance between self-acceptance and self-rejection in our
personalities.

If we must accept ourselves before we can effectively love
others, we also come to understand that love for others is essentially a campaign of build their self-esteem. The husband of
Severine, the prophet Hosea, the Lord loving his people must all
try to persuade the beloved that she is not bad but good. So it
is with us. The one we love has a less than adequate evaluation
of himself. He is afraid to surrender himself to us because he
does not feel adequate to cope with us. He is afraid to be open
with us because he's afraid that we will see him for what he is
really worth. He does not want to run the risk of trusting us
because he does not have the conviction that he is strong enough
to avoid being swept away by the power of our emotions. A
love relationship therefore might be viewed as a morale-building
enterprise in which two people try to persuade each other of
their mutual worth and dignity. When the process works right,
it is marvelous to behold: both lovers make immense gifts and
receive immense rewards and neither loses anything.

Love is also a gigantic leap of faith. The gift of self in love
means that an escape has been made from the tension between
the lover's very high evaluation of us and our own very low
evaluation. We accept more or less as a working hypothesis the
idea that the lover might be right, but our hesitancies, doubts,
and fears do not go away. We simply act despite them. Thus, in
Belle de Jour, the heroine is not able to relinquish completely
her self-punishing fantasies, but the fantasies are no longer
strong enough to separate her from her husband. The act of
giving ourselves to others, despite the persistence of fear of our
own worthlessness, is the critical moral act that a man makes.
It means the difference between an open and a closed human

being. An open human being can grow and expand. A closed human being has cut himself off from his fellowmen.

The act of self-opening and self-surrender in a relationship of love is a profoundly sexual experience and hence the sexual imagery of some of the great mystics is not merely a poetic metaphor. There can be sexual union without interpersonal unity. Many marriages seem to be unions without intimacy, although sex without intimacy and trust is bound to be frustrating and unsatisfactory. But if there can be sex without intimacy, there cannot be intimacy without man's sexuality being involved. When man surrenders himself to love, he surrenders his whole self, his body as well as his spirit. In some relationships the bodily surrender involves the act of marriage, in many others it does not. But there is, nonetheless, a profound commitment of the human body to the one that is loved. We may not fully understand yet the implications of this sexual element in all human friendships, but we are nonetheless unable to escape the fact that the body, as part of the human personality, is inevitably given in some fashion to the other in every love relationship.

It follows, therefore, that another name for self-hatred is shame. The terrifying, paralyzing sensation of shame which results from fear of our own bodies is but a surface manifestation of the far more intense fear of our personal worthlessness. Just as physical shame (and by no means is it limited entirely to women) is an agonizing barrier to unity between husband and wife, so is human shame a barrier to the fulfillment of human love. Severine could not give herself to her husband because she was ashamed. Adam and Eve after their sin were paralyzed by shame.

The complex, intricate web of defense mechanisms we create around ourselves is essentially protection for our shame. Aggressiveness, systematic self-deception, self-pity, aloofness, the compulsive search for attention, desperate seeking for possessions or pleasure or power are all attempts to construct masks so the world around us will not see that we are blushing with shame over our own worthlessness. Fortunate are those among us who know that their masks are masks. They may be able to be persuaded to put them aside. Far too many of us did such a good job of fastening our masks in early life that we are firmly persuaded that they are the reality. We will not even consider the possibility that they are merely masks to hide shame. We will vigorously insist that we have nothing to be ashamed of, that we feel no shame, but only because the shame has been so deeply repressed in our personalities. The mask, for all practical purposes, has become the real self and the real self only barely exists. Presumably hell is something like that.

Salvation is putting aside the mask and engaging in self-disclosure. In the protective warmth of the other's regard for us, we begin to reveal ourselves to him, partly because we are sure that we will convince him how wrong he is to esteem us, and partly out of the faint hope that he may after all be right. The act of self-disclosure is a terrifying experience because we become psychically naked to the other and make it possible for him to ridicule us and reject us. There is also a certain sweetness mixed in with this terror, both because it is a relief to have someone see us as we are and also because we are beginning to suspect that the lover will like us even more after we have disclosed ourself to him.

It is virtually impossible to describe self-disclosure without using imagery that is at least implicitly sexual, since the relationship between psychic nakedness and physical nakedness is so close and the two acts are so similar. Ideally, in marriage they symbolize and reinforce each other. In other relationships psychic nakedness does not imply physical nakedness; but the latter is still a useful image for understanding the former, probably because man's ability to disclose himself to another psychically is ultimately rooted in his ability to combine sex and friendship in marriage. For this reason, many psychologists argue that counseling relationships across sexual lines, while initially more difficult, are also far more effective.

Poets and novelists have worked hard to describe the immensely meaningful and important experience of physical self-disclosure on the wedding night. Whether they have been able to convey adequately its terrors and delights may be doubted. Interestingly enough, however, most of their attempts have focused on the effect of the unveiling experience on the bride, but there is every reason to believe that the experience is at least as terrifying for the husband, particularly since the cultural norms permit her to express her fear and shame but make no such concessions to him. In fact, there is probably far greater prudery among men than among women; no matter how much he may protest to the contrary, it is harder for him to undress in her presence than for her to undress in his. The psychic correlates of this phenomenon are extremely important. Self-disclosure comes more readily to women than it does to men; their culture and their training has prepared them for unveiling. In the short run at least, it is easier for a woman to be open; she is more accessible as a lover and a better patient in therapy. But, in the long run, in our society psychic openness for a woman, like physical openness for her, can easily remain at a superficial level. It is more difficult for a man to begin the process of self-disclosure, but once begun it is not likely that he can stop short of full disclosure. A woman can divorce herself from physical nakedness and easily make it a very superficial gift. A man may hide from the fact of his nakedness, but once he accepts the fact, the gift he gives is much less likely to be superficial. There is reason to believe that the same phenomena occur on the psychological level.

One may pursue the analogies between the two forms of self-disclosure even further. The terrors and the delights of removing one's garments in the presence of one's spouse are equally balanced at the beginning of the marriage, but if the marriage is a healthy and happy one, the terrors recede, though they do not vanish, and the delights increase; the spouses become skilled at forms of self-disclosure which are most rewarding to themselves and to each other, so that in a very real sense they seduce each other to more and more pleasurable physical trust and openness. As they become more sophisticated at the art of physical nakedness, each becomes more persuaded of the beauty and the dignity of his own body. In such happy marriages the bodies of the two spouses, both in the presence of each other and in events of everyday life, display a posture of relaxed confidence which does indeed enhance their attractiveness.

In the same way, psychic self-disclosure becomes easier and more rewarding as it progresses. As we develop the skill and the art of letting our personality expand for another, we become more conscious and more confident in the beauty and the dignity of our personhood and more eager to share this beauty and dignity with those we love and who love us. The experience of self-disclosure is so rewarding that we do our best to create a climate and atmosphere in which others can disclose themselves to us. Just as the spouse has become confident of the value of his own body and is able to commit himself to be attuned to the subtleties of his mate's body, so the personality which has finally discovered its own worth and value is able to be far more attuned to the nuances of other personalities. The process of self-disclosure therefore persuades us through the favorable reaction of another that we do have dignity and value. Furthermore, it actually enhances our dignity and value, both because latent strengths are encouraged and also because we learn how to encourage others' latent strengths.

We have pushed the analogy between physical and psychic self-disclosure pretty far, perhaps embarrassingly far for some more Jansenist readers, but surely no further than the reality of the connection between the two demands. In marriage the two kinds of self-disclosure must be intimately linked. In the absence of psychic self-disclosure, physical self-disclosure will soon become unrewarding. On the other hand, given the burden of the closeness of the marriage union, psychic self-disclosure will normally be extremely difficult if it is not reinforced by the powerful joy of physical union.

But psychic self-disclosure is not limited to marriage, even though it is ultimately rooted in man's capacity for marriage and marriage is the best analogy we have available for understanding it. Self-disclosure outside of marriage is both easier than in marriage and more difficult; easier because it is free from the immense burden of intimacy and intimate responsibility that the family union necessarily implies and more difficult because it lacks the physical ecstasies that marital intercourse can create.

It is fruitless to argue which kind of self-revelation is better. They are both good. They are both part of the human condition. They are both available for everyone, though the marriage union is optional salvation, while psychic openness is indispensable. Neither need interfere with each other, though both may. One's openness to a psychiatrist or a friend may, for example, be impeded by the fear that such openness would interfere with one's marriage, but the openness itself need not do the marriage any harm and in many instances in fact will enhance it.

A number of people have suggested to me that certain elements of the personality which will not develop in the marriage friendship can be developed in friendships outside of marriage and hence reinforce the marriage. The point that these observers make seems to be twofold: first of all, in any marriage relationship, options must be exercised. All dimensions of the personalities of the two partners cannot be developed, but man has an infinite capacity for personality development. Hence elements of his personality which are not stressed in the marriage relationship can be enhanced in other relationships, which, given trust and love between the husband and wife, are not only not threats to the marriage but reinforce it.

Secondly, they seem to be saying that the very fact that one sleeps with another person and rears a family together with that person imposes certain stylistic limitations on the relationship. If the relationship is the only one of trust that the person permits himself, he inhibits the development of somewhat different personality styles. Because of the inevitable demands of marriage and family, there is a certain carefree and superficial style which is not available to the relationship, but which has a value of its own and which may exist in other relationships to the enhancement of the person and the marriage relationship in which he is involved.

These are complex, subtle issues about the nature of human love which mankind is only beginning to investigate. It must be noted that while in the previous paragraphs we spoke of other relationships of love besides the marriage relationship, we were not necessarily limiting these relationships to members of the opposite sex. The possibility implied in these paragraphs is that man can, in addition to his marriage, engage in profoundly meaningful relationships of self-disclosure with other human beings, which is to say that he can enjoy deep and intimate love for and with other human beings.

We've been arguing in this chapter that love consists essentially of the ability to disclose one's self to others, an ability rooted in esteem for ourself. We've also asserted that the act of self-disclosure normally generates self-disclosure from the beloved, thus enhancing both his self-esteem and our own. In some painful and horrendous circumstances, the other is not able to cope with our openness and our honesty. He is not ready or able to hear what we say; his masks are so thick, his defenses so strong, his self-deception so pervasive that he rejects our openness and our honesty. This is an extraordinarily painful experience because it is rejection; we have tried to give ourself to someone else and he is not strong enough to respond. Even though we feel sorry for him for his inability, we are discouraged, humiliated—as would be a spouse whose body is rejected in fear or disgust by his mate. As we become older and more experienced, we tend to judge fairly well who is ready to accept our self-disclosure and who will be frightened by it, but there is still the inevitable element of risk in any act of trust and the possibility of rejection always makes trusting something of a calculated risk.

The selfish person is the one who does not have the courage and the persistence to work at the difficult task of believing in himself and giving himself to others. The selfish person is not the one who loves himself too much, but rather the one who does not love himself enough and is not willing to try to give himself to others. Trust is the ability to believe that one can be loved for what one is and not for what one can do. Trust is not exactly a surrender without fear but it is a surrender in the face of fear, despite fear. One is able to trust because one is confident in one's self and because of such confidence he can take the risk of conceding complete freedom to the other; if the other rejects me, then I am still me and still worthwhile. Alas, such confidence is not easy to come by, and God protect the poor person whose first attempts at self-disclosure are harshly rejected; Heaven also protect the child who by his very childishness begins life in a situation of trust and finds that trust destroyed by harsh, unloving, manipulating parents who value him not for what he is but for what he can do. Most of those who have impenetrable masks, whose self-defense and self-deception are so pervasive that they do not even realize they are self-defense and self-deception, acquired their masks at their parents' knees. Systematic self-deception, systematic denial which leads us to defense mechanisms to protect our shame is, in the strict sense of the word, neurotic and sick.

And the opportunities for hiding are almost infinite. One can pretend to be a "quiet" person, the strong and silent type, but the strong and silent type is generally the weak and timid type who doesn't say much because he is afraid that he has nothing to say. Or we can become moralizers who hide our own fears and desires behind very serious discussions of the moral evil we see around us. Or we can become Don Juans who do not stay in bed with any one person long enough to run the risk of that person getting to know us, but we reassure ourselves into thinking that sexual potency is the same as personal dignity. We can become intellectualizers who hide our inadequacies behind abstract and complex theorizing. Or we can become radicals with an authoritarian approach to social reform which cloaks our own doubts and insecurities. We can become hysterical—in the psychiatric sense of the word—and gain attention for ourselves by pleas for sympathy and compassion, since obviously there is nothing in our personality which merits for us more than compassion. Finally, in this day of pop psychology, we can hide behind counterfeit openness, behind the odd notions of instant honesty and intimacy which provide a not very subtle cloak for aggression.

Given the multiplicity of masks available, how does one begin to put them aside? There must first of all be dialogue; we must begin to talk to others, and more important, listen to them. There must be exploration; we must be brave enough to engage in the act of "discovery" with another. There must be co-operation; we have to be brave enough to work with and for other people. There must be patience; we must try to acquire sympathy for other human beings that enables us to see reality the way they see it. We must also refuse to be a doormat, refuse to let our dignity and our values be abused by others.

And this last point is an extremely important one, particularly since so many of us were taught at one time in our lives that Christianity, real authentic Christianity, demanded that we have no respect for our own dignity and value but rather should turn ourselves over to the arbitrary whims of our superiors and those whom we serve. The Christian must, of course, be ready to sacrifice himself in many ways for others, sacrifice himself on occasion even unto death, but there are some things that no man may give up, some things which are in a very real sense more important than life itself; dignity, self-respect, personal freedom are not commodities that we can sacrifice or should attempt to sacrifice.

There are areas of privacy in our lives which we may not make available to everyone. There are some times when we should not be available to our clients and there are some elements in our lives which ought not to be available to our superiors. If we have a sense of our dignity and our worth, we preserve privacy in certain segments of our time and space, as well as integrity in certain segments of our belief schemes, and no one may violate either this privacy or this integrity. Since such a sense of privacy and integrity makes government somewhat more difficult and also demands more personnel, certain kinds of ecclesiastical leaders in the past have tried to socialize self-respect and integrity out of the personalities of the young people they were training. That it was done in good faith, we may be prepared to concede, but that objectively it was harmless we must vigorously deny.

No man, no matter how high his ecclesiastical office, may violate the privacy and the integrity, the self-respect, the dignity of another man. No man may demand that another be completely available to everyone at all times. Yet to reject these demands requires a concept of one's own value and worth which in many seminary and religious communities was deliberately suppressed and in many high schools and colleges deliberately discouraged. If we do not have enough confidence in ourselves to resist the doormat temptation, then it is to be very much feared that self-disclosure is going to be almost impossible. If we do not respect ourselves enough to protect our integrity and privacy, then we certainly do not respect ourselves enough to disclose ourselves to others.

Despite the immense obstacles that still stand in the way of human love, the opportunity for love in our time is the greatest it has been in all human history. Because we understand so much more now about the dynamics of human relationships, we realize what fear and distrust and suspicion are and we have some insights into how they are to be defeated.

We also understand, though rather dimly, the multitudinous plurality of human love and how foolish it is to speak of love in comparative terms. A "best" friend relationship that is "most important" or that means "everything" is likely to be an unhealthy relationship. Human nature, quite to the contrary, is capable of a polymorphous diversity of relationships which complement and reinforce rather than oppose one another—if we have enough self-confidence and trust to believe in the reality of relationships. It is precisely the paralyzing fear that a relationship will depart from the reality in which it is immersed that causes it to depart from that reality. The great inhibitors of human love are possessiveness and jealousy, both of which are other forms of self-hatred. If a person is confident enough of his own worth, he need not fear that he will lose a love. The very fact that he does not fear it will generally guarantee that he has nothing to fear.

We provide our young people today with a far longer period of time between infancy and adulthood. According to Kenneth Kenniston, in contemporary American society we not only have childhood and adolescence but also a period during early and middle twenties which Kenniston calls "youth," in which young people are free from immediate financial responsibilities and can experiment playfully to discover who they are and what they want. It is during these two periods of adolescence and youth that self-discovery through self-disclosure is most likely to begin for those for whom it is going to begin at all. While it would be a mistake to suggest that most young people take advantage of these opportunities, the opportunities are there. More young people understand the need for trust in self-disclosure than have ever understood it before.

If, however, there are greater opportunities for and greater understanding of love than there have ever been before, there is also a greater necessity for it. Our society is so complex and impersonal that dehumanization can only be resisted by a network of loving relationships more intense and more trusting than the world has ever seen before. Furthermore, while new categories of thought and description may help us understand a little bit better what is involved in the leap of trust, they may not, in the final analysis make it any easier. It is still hard to believe that we are worth loving. Many of us go through life like Severine, punishing and injuring ourselves, partly to gain attention and sympathy, but mostly because of the conviction that that's what we really deserve. Unlike Severine, we do not have enough openness to take the plugs out of our ears and hear people shouting all around us that we are wrong.

It might be asked where in all of this there is room for God. The only reply that is feasible, of course, is that God has been everywhere in this chapter. We can be open to God only by learning openness to our fellowmen. He who does not trust other human beings really cannot trust God; he who professes to trust God must be willing to run the risk of trusting others. Man's hunger for the Absolute is rooted in his hunger for love and affection. His instinct for openness to his fellows is that same instinct which leaves him open to the Almighty. In his fear and his distrust of others, his suspicion that they may "chump" him is the same as his fear that the powers of the universe are going to "chump" him. If we are incapable of intimacy with our fellows, the ultimate reason is that we do not have enough conviction about the goodness of the powers of the universe. This is another way of saying that we do not trust God.

On those whose lives contain no real intimacy, a somber judgment must be made. They do not trust God enough. As we will see in a later chapter, their salvation is not impossible; but it will require a miracle of divine intervention. If there is no intimacy in our lives, then we are less than human and we are turning our backs on the powers of the universe. We had better seek a therapist before it is too late.

3. *Won't This Plane Ever Land?*
(HOPE)

As I said in the introduction to the book, I live, partly by choice and partly by circumstance, on the margins between the Church and academia, a highly vulnerable situation at best. Slight changes in ecclesiastical or educational or governmental policy can erode the somewhat dubious base on which I stand. Furthermore, many of the institutions to which I have deep commitments are in trouble. The Universal Church is rent by a Thermidorian reaction that was as surprising as it was inevitable after the enthusiasm of the Vatican Council. The American Church has, for all practical purposes, become two churches, the official church of the hierarchy and ecclesiastical leadership and the free church of the lower clergy and the concerned and committed laity. The creativity and enthusiasm which has marked my own archdiocese for decades seems, temporarily at least, to have run out of steam. American democracy is in a serious constitutional crisis, more serious because it has been made serious by hard-line leaders of small minorities, by the mass media, and by misinformed and uninformed public opinion. American liberalism has not been able to come up with a social vision to replace that of the New Deal; it is showing sympathy to hard-line radicals, which demonstrates that it has learned nothing from the lessons and the histories of two gentlemen named Joseph—Stalin and McCarthy. Finally, the upper-middle-class Irish, of which I am a part and in whom so much of the future of both the Church and the nation may depend, seem, in their younger manifestations, to be paralyzed by indecision and fear—truly a very un-Irish phenomenon.

I cite these portents of doom because I want to establish that I find it very hard to be hopeful and that when I write on the virtue of hope I am writing on something that causes me a great deal of trouble. One is consoled under such circumstances, of course, by the old adage that things are always darkest before they get totally black. Things are not only bad—they're probably going to get worse. The present times seem to be an era for the hard-liners, and the lunatic fringe have license to run amuck. Those of us who are moderates are fated to be caught in cross fire from the two extremes.

Hope, therefore, is not an easy virtue. Indeed, according to G. K. Chesterton, it is only a virtue at all when the situation is hopeless. Realistically, I suppose we must say the situation has always been hopeless; at the present time it's just more hopeless than usual. But it is not an accident that in these chapters I have somewhat reordered the presentation of the three so-called theological virtues and put hope last. For, in my conception of the three virtues, hope is rooted in faith and love, and if we lack either, then our hope is likely to be frail and pathetic. We can only have hope if we have an interpretive scheme that gives us meaning and if we accept ourselves enough to love ourselves. We can hope if we have commitment to the notion that the universe is good and also to the much more intimate notion that we ourselves are good. I might note that I suspect my problem is not with my own interpretive scheme, which I think is fine, but with my self-acceptance, which still has a long way to go.

How then does a man of hope respond to crisis? He first of all insists on the necessity of keeping his cool, of resisting that orientation (so common with Protestant scholars and Catholic editorial writers) that sees doom portending at every turn of the road. Things may be bad but they're not as bad as the television commentators would want to make them. The riots in our cities, for example, are serious, but not nearly as serious as the riots in the nineteenth century. Our political conventions may be a weird means of choosing a man for the most important elective office in the world, yet they are certainly much better than were the rigged conventions in the nineteenth century; the most rigged one of all, incidentally, was the one that chose Abraham Lincoln; furthermore, even in the recent election, the convention did nominate the candidate who was most popular with the members of his own party. While the crisis in the Church is a severe one, it is a crisis which comes not from apathy, but from enthusiasm; no organization has ever fallen apart because it had too much enthusiasm. Finally, no one in his right mind would write off the Irish merely because they seem to be plagued by self-doubts.

We must therefore be prepared not to believe the worst when we hear it. The man of hope does not confuse his hope with naïve expectations. He is healthily cynical about new developments and hence is rather difficult to disillusion when these new developments don't seem to work out quite as planned. He is also wary of false prophets, that is to say, the men with easy generalizations and simple solutions, so he is not terribly surprised when the messages of the false prophets are proved inadequate. And finally, the man of hope is capable of suspending judgment until the data are in, though I should say in all honesty today, it does not necessarily have to be collected by the National Opinion Research Center.

In the midst of a disturbing situation in which he finds himself, the contemporary man of hope notes that American democracy has survived worse crises, that only a strong nation can afford to run a whole presidential election on such a non-existing issue as law and order, that the Church has survived more serious crises than this one, and that we have learned one lesson from the Protestant Reformation (it doesn't do any good to leave the Church). So the man of hope listens with amusement to Chet Huntley and Dave Brinkley, but is not prepared to think that things are every night quite as bad as these two prophets would lead us to believe. And if he is willing to go up to Mount Sinai to receive the latest revelations of Eric Sevareid, he does so with the full realization that however insightful, even brilliantly, Mr. Sevareid's commentaries have been for the last quarter of a century, the world has still managed to survive.

I hope it is obvious that I am somewhat facetious in these remarks. The root of our hope is not in the stability of American democracy, or even in the vitality of American Catholicism; I am merely arguing that the wise man does not fall back on the ultimate root of his hope until he has to. But there have been many Christians in our time, in Nazi Germany, for example, who had to fall back on the ultimate roots of hope.

And these ultimate roots are twofold; first of all, our belief in the resurrection, and secondly our belief in our own capacity to grow. For if we believe in the resurrection, we believe that death is an illusion, that it does not defeat us, that even if all else is blotted out, we do survive. The values for which we stand will not die; they are part of Christ's redeeming work. We stand on the shoulders of those who came before us and others will stand on our shoulders. Progress does occur toward the Omega, though it is an erratic and at times uncertain progress. We are part of that progress, more a part of it than people have ever been before. We shall live to see its fulfillment, because together with Christ we shall rise.

The resurrection is not for the man of hope a single event to occur at one point in time. It is a constant progress; each day we can die to our fears, our uncertainties, our confusions, our distrusts, our suspicions, and each day we can rise again to openness, confidence, trust, and love. It is never too late to start and, as psychologist Nevitt Sanford has put it, it is never too late to grow. We might say it more strongly: it is never too late to start over again. We must start over again each day and hence each day is a resurrection. We never need be a creature or a slave of the environment unless we give in to it. Even if there is but one day left in our life, that day can still be a day of resurrection.

Despair, then, is at root a form of infidelity and self-destruction. It is the refusal to have faith, it is the refusal to grow, it is the refusal to believe in the world and in one's self, it is the refusal to attempt to love. No wonder that ancient writers called it a sin against the Holy Spirit and the unforgivable sin. The despairing man has closed himself off; as long as he persists in being closed off, growth, love, life, happiness are impossible to him. The man who despairs is an infidel and a hater. It may well be that he is physically or psychically determined to do this, and hence, not responsible. For him, we must believe that God will somehow provide. For us, openness, faith, and love are still possible and we must provide for ourselves.

Just as in the final analysis love for others depends upon love for ourselves, so hope in the world around us depends on whether we have hope for ourselves. We all have a minimum level of hope or we simply could not survive; yet, since hope is rooted in faith and love and faith and love are both rather weak in the personalities of most of us, the hope that sustains us is at best a weak hope; it usually gets weaker as we get older.

Yet if we could understand ourselves and respect ourselves, hope should become stronger and not weaker. The resources of the human spirit are immense. Most of us tragically do not even begin to tap the resources we possess during our life. We are all too conscious of our limitations, our frailties, our weaknesses, but not very sensitive to our strengths and our possibilities. To the extent that we understand our own emotions, we are frequently frightened by their complexity rather than encouraged by their riches.

But in order that our hope be operative, we must come to know ourselves, to understand who and what we are and who and what we can become. At whatever age in life we now stand, we are a combination of heredity and experience that is filled with limitations and filled with possibilities. There is our biological inheritance, something that social science until very recently has been inclined to discount, because it cannot specify any behavior that is genetically determined. Yet some of us are physically stronger than others; some of us have more sensitive nervous systems; and some of us, a greater capacity for work. There are some young people I have encountered who have managed to survive tremendous psychological traumatizations only because of sheer genetic strength. They are fortunate indeed, because others would have gone mad under the same pressures. The biological substratum of our personality is given; we cannot change it and the modifications we can work on it are minor. But we can understand it, adjust to it, and channel the resources that it makes available to us. Above all, we can realize that we must judge ourselves not by other people's physical capacities, but by our own. Unfortunately, the atmosphere of competition in American society, which leads to frequent and minute comparison of children in purely physical terms (before the grading system of academic marks and professional income takes over), leads those who are not physically strong to judge themselves against standards which would be appropriate for those who are.

In addition to our biological substratum, we also have in our personality a residue of the experiences of our emotional development through childhood, adolescence, and youth. We have survived in one fashion or another the discovery that we are distinct from our parents and our parents are not one person, but two persons who have relationships with each other as well as with us. We then managed to get through the shocking discovery that there were other people who also had a claim on our parents—siblings, whom we hated because they received attention which we had assumed was ours by right. Then came the even more rude shock that not everyone in the world viewed us with the same feelings as did our parents and we had to adjust to the much less tender demands of the peer group. In adolescence we then became aware that we were someone distinct from others as a person and that our value and worth could not be taken for granted. We were forced in this process of discover-

ing ourself to take a long, hard look at the values we had
absorbed from our parents and made a part of our world view.
We rebelled a bit, modified the values a bit, and, if we were
fortunate, made a commitment to them that was relatively free.
We then went through a process of differentiating ourself not
merely from the values of our family, but from the values of the
whole of Western culture and individuated ourselves over against
these values, avoiding, if we were fortunate, the perils of alienation from society and alienation from ourself. We faced the
challenge of competency and skill that was demanded of us
first in school and then in the world of profession. And finally,
we took the great risk of attempting to merge our personalities
with other personalities in relationships of affection and love.

It is a difficult and perilous path that we have walked from
birth to our present age. So many mistakes could have been
made by so many people which might have misdirected, maimed,
or frustrated us. Many mistakes were made and many others
were not. The self that emerged is for most of us capable of
functioning more or less effectively, capable of making at least
some choices more or less freely, capable of loving and giving in
love more or less adequately. But not all these experiences from
infancy to adulthood have been negative. We have mastered
some problems; our personality has certain strengths; there are
some things we know we can do and other things we rather
suspect that we might be able to do well if we ever had the
chance to try. We know that from heredity, or environment,
or culture, or education, or a complex combination of all of
them, we have talents and abilities, some of which we have used
and others of which we are afraid to try.

The broad framework of our personality as it has been shaped
by heredity and experience is subject to some modification and,
perhaps through extended therapy, substantial modification. But
even within the present framework there is still room for choice,
for growth, for commitment, for risk taking. Within the limitations under which we must operate there is room for a conscious
decision on where to focus our energies. It is this decision on

the focus of energies which is what many psychologists mean by life project. The project is not the psychological equivalent of building a sailboat or mastering a computer, but it is rather the delineation of those possibilities of personal growth on which we intend to concentrate. Hope is merely the expectation that our life project is worth trying and that we can be moderately successful in it. Despair is not choosing to focus one's energies; it is turning over control of our life project to others so that they can make our decisions for us; it is backing down on the prospects of the life project, engaging in self-deceptions about it. Despair is giving up; it's not trying, becoming complacent in our failure and our mediocrity; it is settling down, arguing that it is already too late for us.

It is never too late in fact for anyone. But it almost is. For us, things are bad and they are getting worse and almost irrevocably worse; but the controlling word here is *almost*—it is always almost too late, but never quite. There is still a chance, there is still time to start over again, but we must do it now before it is really too late. We can, if we are of a mind, curse our fate or scream at the elements or, like the ancient Persian king, lash the sea with chains because we are angry at it. It'll make us feel good for a time but it isn't going to help much. The alternative is one practiced by any ardent supporter of a Chicago athletic team: we must wait until next time and start over again.

The principal enemy of our hope is not so much despair. Most of us have enough genetic strength to avoid complete despair. Our real foe is discouragement, discouragement which crimps our hopes, stifles our expectation, blights our vision, and ruins our dreams, discouragement which causes it to rain on our parades. Discouragement does not tell us we're utterly worthless, but it suggests to us subtly that our life project does not matter, that there is no point in our trying, and that a nice mediocre balance between vision and cynicism is the best way to adjust to the fruitlessness of all human endeavor. The late theologian Gustave Weigel in an uncharacteristic moment of discouragement once said that all things human, given enough time, go badly. Gus did not live that way, and did not die that way; but that he, like all Christians, would feel that way at times is understandable. Things do go badly; discouragement and complacent mediocrity seem to be the counsel of wisdom. Cynicism is such a safe and easy and comfortable way out. Alas, we who believe in the resurrection promise are in no position to take that way out. We can and probably must flirt at times with discouragement, but for the hopeful Christian discouragement as a permanent state is quite inadmissible.

The time I am writing these words I am caught in the midst of my annual late-October depression: the Democrats are going to lose, the computer doesn't work, Mr. Herr isn't very funny, Father Kennedy has vanished on a lecture tour somewhere around the country, my closest friends are even more discouraged than I, my intellectual and ecclesiastical heroes all seem to be in a sad state of disarray. I feel something like a hypocrite (though in truth, not very much) as I write. Yet unfortunately for my discouragement and my desire to escape from the margins, the very repetition of these words about the necessity of hope as a response to the resurrection promise begins to scatter the clouds of discouragement. If one takes a good hard look at what one believes in, it is very difficult to remain discouraged.

The extent to which we can control our discouragements varies from person to person. Some of us exercise such power over our negative emotions that they never get out of control. We therefore can afford the occasional luxury of periods of gloom, self-pity, and black moods; even if they're not very healthy, they are not very destructive. But others of us don't dare let these moods last very long, because they can get out of control and come close to destroying us. The worst fit of discouragement I ever had began on the January day I heard about Cardinal Meyer's brain tumor and lasted into the Holy Thursday liturgy. Looking back on it, it was a black, sick experience, one which I could have stopped early in the game. But after the first couple of weeks it was quite out of control and gripped me in a fashion which in retrospect I can only say was almost physical and organic. I suppose in some deeper level of my personality I didn't want it to go on; otherwise the tremendous hopefulness of the Holy Thursday liturgy would not have blasted me out of it. Yet I am quite sure as I look back that if it had gone on for another week or two I would have been in a hospital, physical or mental, having the scattered pieces of my personality sewed back together again. It was not an experience I would recommend to anyone.

The point of this personal reminiscing is that there are tremendous positive forces at work within the human personality, forces which strain mightily toward the furtherance of our life project. We keep these life forces under check only with great effort. The human race in general and each individual in particular has become quite skillful at developing the talents necessary to rein in the natural hopefulness and optimism of the human personality, but then it takes more psychic effort to repress our hope than it does to repress our sexuality. Both are manifestations of the life instinct, both are profoundly human; but hope reaches out beyond the limitations of humanness in a fashion sexuality does not and hence is, if anything, the more powerful of the two. Repress it we can, but it is difficult and, what is more, foolish.* The life project into which we focus our energies, then, is rooted in hope, just as hope in its turn is rooted in faith and in love. We do not pursue our life project with the expectation that it will be completely successful—not, at least, if we have any experience at all—but we still pursue it, because of our hope, with the expectation that it will be somewhat successful and perhaps more successful than we have any reasonable right to think it will be. In other words, if we are men of hope, we never stop trying.

For the Christian, the life project takes on another dimension; his hope is more solidly grounded than the hope of the

* Or perhaps sexuality and hope are but different manifestations of one human drive—the drive to become more than one is.

non-Christian; it also gives force to the life project, which makes great demands on our resources. We who are Christians are committed not only to fulfilling ourselves, not only to the extension of our talents and energies, not only to the giving of our enriched selves in enriching love to others, we are also committed to spreading the good news.

The good news is both continuous and discontinuous from the human condition. On the one hand, it asserts that which man in his better moments is inclined to believe anyhow, namely that the world is good, the higher powers of the universe are gracious, and death is an illusion. But on the other hand, the good news asserts these truths on the basis of a highly special dimension in human history—the theophany in Jesus of Nazareth and a continuation of that theophany in the Christian people. It further asserts, far more blatantly than man would have dared to hope, that death leads but to resurrection. The simultaneous continuity and discontinuity of the good news with the human condition is such that it is both a fulfillment of humanistic strivings and a promise of a transcendence far beyond these strivings. The Christian then, as we said earlier, is a man on the margins, fully committed to the human effort and yet committed to something which is far beyond human effort. He is an outsider and yet the nature of his outside commitment is such that he must immerse himself totally in the inside. The dilemma of transcendence vs. the incarnation is built into the relationship between the good news and the human condition and no amount of theologizing will explain it away.

Nevertheless, the paradox need not inhibit the Christian, for he has, as Brian Wicker pointed out, merely the humanist who has a greater degree of certainity of the ground on which he stands. That which transcends the human condition is fortunately, from a Christian's viewpoint, not opposed to it. The good news, while it may transcend our life project, reinforces it instead of negating it. Since the Christian must spread the good news in his life, he has stronger motivation for applying himself to his life project and greater hope in times of difficulty and discouragement. The Christian spreads the good news, not as Cardinal Suhard has observed, by engaging in propaganda, but rather by engaging in the kinds of faith and love that others will envy. "By this shall all men know you that you are my disciples, that you have love for one another."

It is therefore in the depths of commitment to his interpretative scheme, in the abandon of his self-disclosure and self-giving, and in the dedication to his life project that the Christian announces the good news. His hope is more powerful because his faith is stronger and his love more trusting. And faith, hope, and love combined together guarantee the fulfillment of his destiny; he will not turn around to put his hand back on the plow.

The Christian is then not an alienated man. He is neither alienated from himself, nor from others, nor from the world around him. The conviction that goodness can overcome and the confidence of his self-surrender make him in ideal circumstances the most integrated of men. Because of the powers of his commitment and conviction and surrender he ought to be better at everything that he does than the man who does not have his perspective but has the same kind of talents. If he is a teacher, he should be more available to his students. If he is a researcher, more vigorous in the pursuit of truth; if he is a businessman, more imaginative and ingenious in his work—as well as more honest. If he is a professional man, his standards should be higher and his care for his clients, more generous. If he is a parent, his relationship to his children should be more reassuring and open. If he is a spouse the generosity and the pleasurableness of his love should be more intense. The Christian is a man more passionate in his pursuit for peace, more determined in his quests for racial justice, more resolute in his attempt to create human community, more rigorous in his sensibility, more enthusiastic in his causes, and more hilarious in his joys.

I certainly am not asserting that all Christians are this way, but I *am* saying that the good Christian compared to the good man who is not a Christian has committed himself to these goals because of the special nature of his faith and his love and his hope. To the extent that he does not live up to these goals, he fails to respond to the good news and fails to bring it to his fellowmen. If one is to judge Christianity, one must judge it not by its failures, which are many, but by its successes, which are few and splendid.

While hope is rooted in faith and in love, it is essential that these two other virtues continue to be operative. If we lose our hope, the vision of graciousness which our faith provides us is likely to grow dim, and the confidence and the self-acceptance with which we give ourself to love is likely to be quieted by discouragement and fear of rejection. The battle against discouragement is constant, we *almost* lose every day, but we need not lose. If we do, it is because the good news seems too good to be true and we prefer to be narrow, cynical, discouraged men, lest we be thought fools for believing something that is too good to be true.

4. Wine for My Horses and Food for My Men
(TEMPERANCE)

When we hear the word temperance, we are likely to conjure up an image of a dull, self-righteous, moralizing old maid who has channeled all the goodness urges into hypocrisy and vindictiveness. We think of her going around trying to prevent others from enjoying food or drink or card playing or dancing or sex. She is a distant cousin of the Irish monsignor who used his thorn stick to break up crossroad dances. Her nose is blue, her brow is furrowed, her body is lean and haggard, and she is *against*.

We might recast the public image of temperance in the form of Ken Kesey (in Tom Wolfe's *Electric Kool-Aid Acid Test*) trying to persuade the acid heads of San Francisco that the time has come to go beyond acid and that man indeed ought to be able to "turn on" without acid. Temperance is not the virtue which inclines us to be "up tight," but rather, the virtue which demands that we "let go." It is virtue which impels man to enjoy himself and the world in which he is a part; it demands he be playful, joyous, and devoted to pleasure. If we must think of temperance in any color, I should much prefer to think of it as red rather than blue.

One of the most maddening writers of contemporary times is

Norman O. Brown. His books are contentious, pedantic, and filled with the dry academicism which he attacks. His devotion to Freud is piously complete. His conclusions do not follow from his reasoning and his sweeping indictments of everything in the past are monstrously unjust. Yet with all these criticisms, one still must concede his essential point: society has an incredible hang-up over pleasure. The hang-up affects society even as influenced by Christianity, whose stand on pleasure ought to have been made perfectly clear by the miracle at Cana and by its constant and pervasive sexual imagery. The Christian who feels guilty when he enjoys a glass of good red wine or the body of his woman (or the body of her man) is not a good Christian.

Brown's analysis has to be looked at if we're going to try to understand the relationship between temperance and pleasure. He argues that physical pleasure in a child is not "genitally organized"; that is to say, it is not oriented toward intercourse, or procreation. It is, rather, "polymorphously perverse"; that is to say, the nervous and sensory systems of children and infants are such that their ability to experience pleasure pervades their entire personalities and is not limited to certain organs at certain times. One need only look at a happy and contented child to realize how simple and undifferentiated and how profound his enjoyment of quite simple pleasures is.

Brown suggests that as we learn to fit into society, we suppress our quest for pleasure and, in the process, dehumanize ourselves. He quotes with approval the aphorism of another psychiatrist, Sandor Ferenczi, "Pure intelligence is a product of dying, or at least of becoming mentally insensitive and is therefore, in principle madness."

One need not accept Brown's indictment of society completely, but it's hard to escape his contention that socialization as it now takes place does seem to squeeze virtually all capacity for enjoyment out of us. Indeed, it frequently destroys much of one's capacity to enjoy the sexual act, into which, in Brown's analysis, the remnants of one's capacity for pleasure have been focused and organized.

Socialization would be a necessity in any society and the pleasure principle, Brown and Jacques Rousseau notwithstanding, is not a feasible norm for organizing human behavior, but the same elements in the socialization process which destroy our self-esteem and crimp our hope also severely damage our capacity for enjoyment.

Furthermore, enjoyment and pleasure have been viewed with great suspicion by most of the world's major religions. The reason is simple enough. The world religions, with the exception of Christianity, Judaism, and Islam, view man as a spirit who is entrapped in the body. The spirit is good, the body is evil. Pleasure and enjoyment are bodily functions and therefore contribute to the imprisonment of the spirit. The Christian stance against this kind of nonsense is clear enough. Man is not spirit, but he is body and spirit combined and the body is redeemed as well as the spirit. The whole of the material world is destined for resurrection through the human body. Jesus attended feasts and drank wine, he worked a miracle to prevent a party from collapsing, sexual imagery abounds in the Judeo-Christian tradition. It is far more pervasive in its sacred books than in the sacred books of any other religion, including Islam, despite the latter's somewhat bizarre notion of the hereafter.

Christianity has not escaped completely the human condition. At times it almost seems that Manicheism has overcome Judeo-Christian respect for the body and its pleasures. Certainly the contemporary fixation of the Catholic Church on the birth control issue to the exclusion of virtually every other aspect of that which Sidney Callahan, author of *Beyond Birth Control*, has called the sexual renaissance is deplorable; but it is deplorable because it misses the best in its own tradition.

The notion then that pleasure is, if not evil, at least to be distrusted is pre-Christian in its origins and has survived despite Christian doctrine and to some extent has even prevented Christians from seeing the implications of their own doctrine. Furthermore, modern capitalism (by modern, one means up until the beginning of the twentieth century) has brought to a new peak of refinement the idea that pleasure must be put off as long as possible. Sober, somber, stolid Calvinists (some of whom are Irish Catholics) built the modern industrial world by repressing all pleasure and most humanity out of their lives and the lives of as many other people as possible. They may have been an evolutionary necessity or, perhaps more appropriately, an evolutionary regression. Middle-class repression of enjoyment and pleasure was, for a long time, taken to be the basic moral core of American society and indeed most of the societies of the North Atlantic community. It was also assumed—as Dr. Brown assumes—that this bourgeois repression of the pleasure principle was Christian in its origin, but it might be better to say that it was Protestant, though clearly most of the great Protestant thinkers, including John Calvin himself, would have rejected it. The Manichees didn't disappear in the fourth century.

Yet the attempt to eliminate pleasures from human life—at least as much as one possibly can—is, if we stop to think about it, ludicrous. Man can no more stop enjoying his body or other people's bodies than he can stop breathing air. A blue sky, a cool drink, the sound of music, a female form (the male form, too, for that matter)—all of these are going to bring man pleasure, even though he may fiercely try to avoid it and feel very guilty about the little enjoyment he does receive; he may even feel the necessity of justifying it in terms that it is good for his business.

Pleasure is rooted in man's animality, which, if you happen to be a puritan, is enough to make it bad without any further discussion, but if you happen to be a Christian, it doesn't bother you because you realize that animality in humans means the same thing as humanity. Pleasure is simply the experience that man has when he comes into physical contact with the enjoyable aspects of his environment. To reject or repress pleasure is to deny either the goodness of man's body or the goodness of the world with which one comes into contact. In the Christian tradition, both alternatives are untenable.

Physical pleasure at root is an ecstatic experience and in that, it forces us to be aware of the reality beyond ourselves and to acknowledge that that reality is good. The ecstasy may be very minor or it may shake the fibers of our being. Most pleasures are somewhere in between, but however intense they may be, they represent rewarding contacts with external reality and imperiously demand that we abandon our attempts to isolate ourselves inside the walls of our own intellectuality and cut ourselves off from all contact with the physical world. But no matter how much we try to resist, no matter how much we aspire to the nirvana of the oriental mystic, pleasure seeks us out, shakes us, immerses us once again in our human and animal condition. Pleasure can, of course, become selfish. It can become the occasion for hurting or ignoring others, but at root pleasure is an antidote to selfishness, because it forces us to share our bodies and ourselves with the rest of the world. Pleasure pours in and opens us up to the world even if we do not want to be so open, it overwhelms our selfishness, our narrowness, our fear and cynicism; all too frequently we seem to do everything in our power to resist seduction and to isolate ourselves dispite its attractions.

The Christian's critical question is not the legitimacy of pleasure or enjoyment, but rather, the co-ordination of pleasure with the other goals of human life. Here he has to part company with Norman Brown. He fails to see how Eros by itself can provide us with the norms for respecting other persons. It is also unlikely that the wisdom of the Stoic who realized that the unlimited pursuit of pleasure is disastrous for the personality can be written off as merely a sophisticated form of repression. Norman Brown seems to equate a limitation on the focusing of human energies with "organization" and repression, but limitation is essential for the integration of the personality. For if the personality remained polymorphously perverse, it would be merely a formless blob. The question the Christian must ask is how a balance can be struck between the personality integration required of an adult and the spontaneous (if not polymorphous) ability to enjoy pleasures of the child. There ought not to be a contradiction between the playful spontaneity of the child and an intelligent focusing of personal resources of the adult. As a matter of fact, one could even go so far as to say that a critical element in adult maturity is the ability freely and spontaneously to enjoy a great deal of pleasure.

The question may be easy enough to answer in theory but in practice a tendency to swing from the libertine extreme to the puritan extreme without being able to strike a balance seems to be very powerful. The libertine does not seem to be enjoying his pleasure principle. Perhaps the two of them are brothers under the skin. Neither of them is willing to face inevitable tensions.

Man is an animal and his animality is good. He also transcends his animality and pleasure is therefore appropriate when it reinforces rather than impedes his quest for self-transcendence. Temperance, I take it, is a virtue which enables a man freely and spontaneously to enjoy pleasure, because he recognizes that his pleasure is ordained toward self-transcendence.

But if traditional Christian asceticism has made a mistake on the matter of pleasure, it has surely not been in the direction of insisting too much on it. One must note that this is most unfortunate, because, as John Hotchkin has remarked in his brilliant article in *The Critic* on the "Christian Meaning of Flesh," puritanism is a far more pervasive and dangerous enemy than libertinism. Few people are libertines, if only because they cannot afford it, but most people, including most Christians, are not able to give themselves over unreservedly to healthy pleasure. The polymorphous perversity of childhood has not been integrated into an adult personality, it has been repressed out of existence. For most men, the Christian message is not so much one of self-restraint as it is of self-liberation. Ken Kesey, Timothy Leary, and the other high priests of psychedelia are closer to being right in their critique of modern middle-class society than are those zealous souls who go around the drugstore magazine racks trying to remove magazines with dirty pictures. Hugh Hefner, with his notion that pleasure ought to be playful, is closer to the truth than the seminary spiritual advisors who urged upon us custody of the eyes. Hefner and the psychedelics

are wrong only because the totally undisciplined playfulness of
sensuality which they advocate is ultimately self-destructive.
One simply cannot get away from the stoics; pleasure must be
limited if it is to be enjoyed; but limitation does not mean that
pleasure is to be feared or repressed or denied or justified on the
grounds that it helps one's business. It merely means that it must
be seen in the context of the whole life project of the total
personality.

Most of us, then, need the virtue of temperance so that we
may be able to enjoy ourselves and enjoy the world in which
we live. One is astonished, for example, to realize that even
though the human body is obviously made to be played with,
few husbands and wives can engage in such playfulness with any
degree of skill, relaxation, or taste. On the contrary, playfulness,
such as it may be, tends to be serious, slightly morbid and
tinged with shame and guilt; not much in the way of gratitude,
one must say, to the God who made the human body so delightful and delight-giving.

Similarly, the world in which we live is filled with pleasurable
sights, sounds, smells, and sensations, and yet we have so many
more important things to do that we rarely pause to savor these
pleasures and when we do, we feel terribly guilty about it. The
Church condemns the abuse of sex and quite rightly so, but
perhaps also it should condemn the equally ungrateful abuse of
the other pleasures of the world: air pollution, water pollution,
or even worse, the casual unawareness of the goodness and the
beauties of the material world that afflicts so many Christians.

In the many complex issues involved in the question of the
role of pleasure in human life, the mere assertion that pleasure is
good and to be encouraged does not solve the problem of
whether certain kinds of pleasure are functional or dys-functional
for the integration of the personality and the furtherance of
one's life project. It is reasonably clear that the concern about
"lustful" thoughts which seems to have obsessed many earlier
writers was misplaced. This is not to say that certain kinds of
sexual fantasies are not harmful (they clearly are), but it is to

say that a spontaneous reaction of delight for a beautiful person of the opposite sex, or indeed for one of one's own sex, is normal and healthy and not the sign of moral perversity. Furthermore, the moral theology manuals that viewed all physical exchanges of affection as "approximate occasion of mortal sin" clearly missed something important about the role of touch in human life. Kissing and embracing are means of communication between human beings.

The body can send messages of openness and encouragement which the human voice is unable to express. I am not suggesting that physical affection is appropriate under every circumstance and between every two persons who encounter one another, but I am suggesting that the powerful exchange of affection in an embrace is, under certain sets of circumstances, not only appropriate but almost demanded by the situation.

If temperance is that virtue which enables us to enjoy physical pleasures, it also is the virtue which enables us to keep in good repair the organism through which physical pleasure is received; that is, the human body. Modern man is particularly perverse on the subject of his body. He pampers it, fills it with medicine, protects it from heat and cold, anoints, perfumes, and cleans it—perhaps more than any of his predecessors would have deemed decent—yet he drives it too hard, lets it get overweight and sloppy, refuses to heed its signals of weariness and fatigue, and frequently behaves in the face of illness either like a hypochondriac or a Christian Scientist. One would like to be able to say that the current cult of "jogging" is a sign that the health and vitality of the human body is once more being respected, but the attitude of many of the joggers leaves one to suspect that the goal of their exercise is not so much the well-being and attractiveness of their physical person but rather a compulsive and frantic attempt to replace one form of intemperance with another.

There are many obscurities in our understanding of the implications of physical affection and indeed many other obscurities in our understanding of the meaning of pleasure in human life.

We have only very recently begun to understand that pleasure is an indispensable dimension of human living and makes an indispensable contribution to personality growth. We are not yet at ease with these facts and it's going to take us time to sort out the puzzle from the confusion, to establish wisdom which will make us able to distinguish authentic and healthy pleasure instincts from unhealthy self-deception. But, despite these qualifications, the Christian must insist that the virtue of temperance compels him to say that pleasure is a good thing and that we, if we are to be fully human, must have more of it rather than less.

One need only look to the contemporary middle-class professional man to realize what an intemperate man he is. See him, for example, at a weekend in the country: he arrives late on Saturday afternoon, because of course he's had to finish up some things at the office on Saturday morning; he paces restlessly around the house for a few moments and then pounces eagerly on the Saturday newspaper, which he devours—perhaps even twice. He then descends to the beach, perhaps even going so far as to take off his coat and roll up his sleeves, though he will hardly remove his tie. He throws stones at the water, thus reasserting his masculinity by demonstrating that he still can skip the stones off the waves; he may even somewhat listlessly toss a football or a softball back and forth with another of his species. Sunday he sleeps late, stares moodily at his cigarette during breakfast, reads all the Sunday newspaper comprehensively, perhaps even twice, pays another ritual visit to the beach, takes a nap, eagerly watches the baseball game on television, and then leaves early because he wants to beat the traffic on the way home. He cannot play, he cannot relax, he surely cannot commune with nature or with his fellow human beings and yet is quite puzzled after such a weekend of restless indifference why his wife is not particularly receptive to him in the marriage bed on Sunday night. He drinks too much, he smokes too much, he eats too much, he can only have "fun" when he's drunk or when he's surrounded with enough of his own kind so that he can pass all the free time talking shop. The telephone is his constant ally, because it enables him to keep in touch with his profession; he is out of shape physically and he is restless in the presence of any of the fine arts, which are nice, but take too much time that he should be spending on the job.

I know of one young M.D. who, on the only night off he had all week, excused himself from a delightful dinner conversation because he "had" to get back to the hospital to see what was happening. It is nice to be all that indispensable, but one suspects that when this young man is flat in bed with a heart attack or incarcerated in a sanatorium, the hospital will function just as well. In fact, the whole world is going to go on functioning as well or as ill as it does now when all the present compulsive professionals have been removed from the scene. If they would be able to abandon their compulsions on the morrow, the world would operate just as smoothly or just as roughly as it is operating at the present.

The professional man has no humor, he cannot relax, he cannot professionally laugh about himself. His moods vary from hyperactivity to hyper-responsibility to irrational excess without ever pausing in between. Since humanity does not exist in the professional man himself, there is reason to expect that his son or his daughter will hie themselves off to the latest center of psychedelia and there compulsively let go. What the professional family cannot accomplish in one generation it will surely accomplish in two. The professional man is intemperate. He can't let go and dies shortly after retirement.

The professional man (and the professional woman) must learn to enjoy life. He must slow down; and golf, jogging, or skiing are not necessarily means of slowing down or indeed occasions for enjoyment. The clever professional can turn his recreation into a professional obligation and make it every bit as unenjoyable as anything else. (Clergymen are, in this respect, as much inclined to professionalism as anyone else. I will leave it to my friends to describe how compulsive I can be about water skiing.)

He must have enough confidence in himself to realize that

his professional success does not require total and compulsive dedication of his person to his career. On the contrary, he must come to understand that such irrational, intemperate, and non-human obsession with the world of work is very likely to be dys-functional to his career. He would be better at his profession if he could let himself be a human person. The "totally committed" professional may be an extremely clever technician, but when he's holding a scalpel or defending me in court, I want to be sure that he is something more than just a technician.

So the professional and his wife must be able to enjoy the surging waters of the lake, the never-ending fascinations of André Malraux's invisible museum, exercise, conversation, games (and not merely those to be observed in the picture tube), vacations, laughter, good food, good wine, and good sex. To the extent that they cannot do so, they must be classified both as intemperate and un-Christian.

And in passing one must extend sympathy to the wife of the professional man; he is a terrible lover. He has linked his masculinity to professional success; since that success is always just around the corner, he is always something less than confident of his masculinity. A male who is insecure in his masculinity is hardly much fun for his wife. He will alternately steer away from sex or make each act of love a test in which he can prove himself; for after all, what is life but a series of tests? The wife ceases to be a person and becomes an object. There are occasional bursts of spectacular passion between them, more frequent experiences of frustration and inadequacy, and most frequent of all, casual indifference. The indifference in its turn is justified by the argument that he is too busy to be able to shower a lot of love and affection on his wife, but he doesn't have to anyhow, because she knows that he cares for her without his having to say it and that she also knows that all his work is for his wife and children in any case. The suburban wife seeking affection and consolation elsewhere is probably more common in fiction than in fact, but one suspects this is principally because other possible sources of affection do not appear very often. The professional man's wife is not very expressive as a lover, either. She yields her husband to the enticements of the stern mistress of his career without much of a fight, and upon some occasions she even encourages him. Neither one of them is very much of a lover; both are quite intemperate.

If the professional man and his wife are to become human beings, if they are to become Christians, they must drastically change the style and the posture of their lives. They must give themselves over to pleasure and not the harassed pleasure that can be generated only when one has enough martinis in one's bloodstream. I suspect that many professional men (and their wives) are going to need prolonged counseling before they are able to accomplish the change.

The alternative to pure rationality is not pure irrationality but a complex synthesis of rationality and non-rationality. The synthesis is not optional, since the man who becomes purely rational ends up being quite irrational. The pure scientists of Hitler's Germany experimented on other human beings in the concentration camps and the purely rational dedicated professional man acts most irrationally when he allows his career to consume him, destroy his capacity for pleasure and his capacity for growth.

The danger for most modern-day American Christians is not that they will be too irrational, but that they will be too rational. One denies the non-rational in man at considerable peril. Both the hyper-rational, that is to say, the mystical, and the infrarational, that is to say, the animal, are integral parts of the human personality. Reason reigns over them as an absolute tyrant, only at the risk of having these two gigantic forces unite against it and overthrow it. The psychedelic revolution and the emerging hippie community are a bizarre combination of the mystical and the animal in revolt against the scientific and the purely rational. Reason, if it is to reign at all, must reign as a constitutional monarch, granting full representation to both the animal and the mystic in man.

Pure rationality is indeed madness; attempts to come as close

as possible to pure rationality run the risk of producing madness
—either the madness of the professional man destroying himself
and his family for the sake of his foolish career or the opposite
madness of the professional man flipping his traces and engaging
in adolescent infidelity in his middle years. Thomas Aquinas,
whom Norman Brown does not quote, asserted somewhere or
the other that man could not live long without pleasure. Modern professional man gives it the good old college try, however,
and succeeds even in making his occasional bursts of pleasure as
non-pleasurable as possible. He is thoroughly convinced that
he is a very temperate person; better that he were a drunk.

Most of what we have said in this chapter would be true even
if the theophany in Christ had not occurred, though it seems
unlikely that the world would have discovered the growth potential of human pleasure if it had not been for the Christian
theophany. The idea that ecstasy takes man out of himself and
opens him up in love and faith and hope to others is by no
means a Christian monopoly, but the idea that the union between God and his people is a pleasurable union comparable to
marriage is uniquely Christian.

The unique contribution that the Christian tradition has to
make to man's pursuit of pleasure is rooted in the good news
that life triumphs over death and that pleasures do not end but
only begin with resurrection. Here the Christian definitely parts
company with Norman Brown, who tries desperately and un-
successfully to make death look like a good thing. This is, of
course, the best the pagan can do. The Christian, being surer
of the ground on which he stands, knows better; death is a bad
thing, it is an evil; fortunately it is an evil which is also an
illusion. The Christian, rooted as he is in the human condition,
can understand the anguished pride of the poet Ovid in his
mistress' arms, *"lente, lente, currite noctis equi."** Ovid was
caught short in his enjoyment of pleasure because he knew
it would end; he knew the steeds of night would eventually

* "Oh slowly, slowly run, ye steeds of night."

bring the dawn of the day when *he* would end. But the Christian has the good news that is too good to be true: it isn't going to end!

Hence he enjoys his pleasure far more than anybody else, because he knows it's only a hint of the good things to come. Christian temperance is rooted not in fear, not in prudery, not in abandonment, not in a desperate search for pleasure that will all too soon be lost, but rather, in anticipation—anticipation of a Promise to be fulfilled.

5. *Where Did All These Other Guys Come From?*
(JUSTICE)

We argued in the previous chapter that temperance was not a puritan virtue and that one of the risks of treating temperance as though it were puritan was that puritanical repression easily generates the opposite extreme. If Temperance is a prude, she is a prude who can readily turn into a *Playboy* fold-out. Similarly, there is great risk in viewing justice as a sober, stern judge who impartially metes out a cold and impersonal equity. A justice of this sort can easily generate a violent opposite reaction. The stern and sober judge can lose touch with humanity and turn into a leader of a gang of clever criminals.

When we were younger we learned that justice was opposed to charity, that it manifested itself in complex rules which told us, for example, in what order we should throw the members of our family out of a sinking boat. As I remember it, the stranger went first, then the acquaintance, then the friend, then the relative, then the parent, and then the child, and then the spouse. We were also advised on who owned the calf if my cow mated with your bull and what compensation you had to render to me for the apples in my orchard which happened to fall into your field. We were further provided with a detailed set of regulations on when and to whom we should pay back the things we had stolen. We were also equipped to cope with the case of the man who defrauded the prostitute (he was not bound to restitution). We were told, though warned against preaching it, that there was no obligation to pay income tax and, under certain circumstances, it was all right to bribe public officials, advice which may have been fine in seventeenth-century society but could be absolutely deadly in contemporary society. It never occurred to the moral theologians that the very fact that it was unwise to preach about one of their conclusions suggested that the conclusion might long since have become outmoded.

We were also taught, though again warned against speaking about it in public, that under certain circumstances a spouse might have intercourse with her husband even if a birth control device was used if failure to do so would lead to serious harm to herself or her children, but she was to be warned against enjoying the act. Exactly what that meant, nobody ever figured out.

Presumably the laity were not given quite so "sophisticated" a version of moral theology, but the textbooks used in the colleges and high schools had the same narrow tyrannical approach to justice, an approach which led one contemporary of mine to remark that moral theology is the art and science of replacing the Sermon on the Mount.

I have no desire to get involved in the controversy over situation ethics.

My concern in this chapter is, rather, with salvaging the underlying principle of the virtue of justice—that principle which says we ought to give to everyone what is his due. The justice I describe may be rather different from the justice of the moral theologians, even the modern ones. All that I can say is that we are speaking about two different, though perhaps related, realities. The kind of human disposition about which I wish to talk in this chapter is not at all opposed to charity. It asserts that everyone has a claim on our charity and that that which is due to people is that we love them.

I should like to conceive of justice as that quality of the human personality which enables us to make the proper disposition of our resources. It is that dimension of the human character which enables us to balance the demands of family, friends, city, church, God, playfulness, contemplation, and career. If the moral theology books do not know of these problems, it may be because the "time problem" is a relatively new discovery in human behavior. In the world of which the moral theology books wrote, under-commitment was the problem, but in the contemporary world it is over-commitment. For the average middle-class American is far too busy, tries to do far too much, and takes on far too many responsibilities. He is a free-floating mass of obligations; as he tries to meet his responsibilities to all his obligations, he usually manages to fail in most of them.

Justice, in my sense of the word, is that virtue which helps us to see some sense of order and priority in the various obligations which we face. It certainly does not provide us with a hard-and-fast set of rules, nor a time schedule, nor a set of detailed instructions on how to decide whether to go to a party or to stay home with the children. At best it gives us a certain sensitivity to ourselves and to our milieu. It enables us to know empirically when we have lost our balance and are putting too much emphasis on one dimension of our complex and demanding lives.

The greatest single violation against justice in modern society is over-commitment to one's career, be that in the world of profession or of homemaking. We pointed out in the last chapter how the career compulsion devastates man's playfulness and his capacity for pleasure and enjoyment and thus impedes the "opening out" experience which pleasure generates. But the career does more than just cause us to cheat ourselves, it causes us to cheat all of the other obligations that are inherent in the network of relationships of which we are a part. The demands which our culture makes on us if we are to be committed to our career are such that we can cheat in all other relationships, not only without much in the way of guilt feelings, but with considerable pleasure in our own moral righteousness. Sacrifice of anything else for the good of the career is considered to be virtuous.

We have been trained for this from our earliest days; our culture demands success. The measure of a man's ultimate worth is his success in his career, just as the measure of a woman's worth is her success as a homemaker and rearer of children. The culturally imposed demands for success are so strong in fact that they are frequently self-defeating. Men with great talent and excellent training frequently produce far below their capacities because they are paralyzed by fear; they are not sure that they are "going to make it," at least not make it up to the level that their internalized pride system demands. They are no good unless they are fantastically successful; hence, rather than settle for the very considerable success of which they are capable, they under-achieve and devise all manner of skillful excuses for such under-achievement. To throw themselves completely into a task and not to achieve the absolute pinnacle of success is far worse a fate than to be mediocre but have good excuses.

Similarly, given the large number of labor-saving devices available to the middle-class housewife, the sloppy and disorderly state of many of their homes is explicable only as a result of neurotic fear. Being a competent housewife is so terribly important that one dares not risk success in it, for then one would have no excuses. It is much better to be sloppy and to demand pity and sympathy for one's incompetency than to run the risk of the commitment of one's self that competent effort would involve. A marriage between a woman whose self-evaluation depends upon her skills in keeping a neat house and a man whose self-evaluation depends upon rapid and dramatic professional success is not likely to be much fun for either of them, or, for that matter, for their children. Yet there are millions of such marriages in our American society; one might almost say that they are typical of the professional classes of our society.

The most serious problem in such marriages and perhaps the most difficult challenge for my virtue of justice is money. Money is the measure of success and the way we use our money demonstrates the authenticity and the permanency of our success. Ours is a competitive culture and the best way to measure success in the competition is to use the handy decimal scale provided by annual income. Now, fortunately or unfortunately as the case may be, the Internal Revenue Service does not make available rank orderings of the population according to income (though some Catholic parishes apparently still rank parishioners according to annual contributions). Thus we must judge another's income by his "standard of living"—by the amount of consumer goods with which he surrounds himself and which he may even occasionally use. Good old-fashioned greed, the inclination to pile up material things, is reinforced in American society by the fact that material possessions enable us to persuade ourselves and others that we rank rather high on the comparative scale of value.

The result of all this is that the typical American middle-class professional man persistently and consistently lives beyond his means. As one young wife put it to me, "It really doesn't matter how much money we make, we always spend a couple of thousand dollars more than we make." We have, therefore, the incredible phenomenon of a society which is the most affluent that the world has ever seen, hung up in a situation where most of its highly trained professional class never have quite enough money. It is strange and bizarre that the most serious conflict in the majority of middle-class marriages is over the use of money, even though these marriages have available more money than did almost any previous marriage in the history of mankind.

The approach of many married couples to money oscillates from one extreme to another, either a rigid budget which provides no room for spontaneity or freedom, or a complete absence of anything approaching rational planning in the use of money. We have again the phenomenon described in the last chapter—hyper-rationality is merely the reverse side of the coin of irrationality and one generates the other.

It ought not to be terribly difficult to handle money rationally, yet freely, particularly in a society where there is so much of it available. If most of us either compulsively save it or compulsively lose control of it, one must surmise that there is something radically and profoundly wrong in our attitudes toward the coin of the realm and toward the self who makes use of the coin. There is a great deal of self-hatred and self-punishment in our relationship to money. For many, it is something too big to handle, something that is so important that it is frightening. It is much bigger than the self. Hence, terrified by the power and importance of money, we overreact, either by pretending that there are no limitations on money or by compulsively worrying about where the money is going.

There are many extreme manifestations of our fear of money; the inveterate gambler who always loses and the inveterate debtor who never quite manages to pay off his old debts before contracting new ones are very sick people, but the neurotic is normative in American society and serious problems with finances are the rule rather than the exception. Money is a hang-up and a weird one at that. Since we have more of it than anyone else has ever had, we ought to be able to enjoy more things, but since we are both afraid of money and compulsively spend it, the things we spend it on are not very enjoyable.

It is all very self-defeating and self-punishing and self-hating. We surround ourself with luxury largely, one fears, because luxury is a way of asserting our value vis-à-vis our neighbors', then feel guilty about the money we have spent in the luxury and are unable to enjoy it. Worse still, the luxury can become an obligation; if we spent all this money on our swimming pool, then we really have to use it whether we like to or not; by the very fact that the swimming pool has become an obligation, it is no longer much fun. So we don't use it and feel guilty about not using it and feel that we ought to use it. Thus the obligation grows bigger, the guilt grows bigger, the fear grows bigger, and the enjoyment and the pleasure decline to zero. After a while we hate the darn swimming pool and wish we could get rid of it. It may seem like a long way from the old moral theology textbooks to the proper use of a swimming pool. The authors of the treatise *De Justitia* probably would not have known exactly what a swimming pool was and if they did they would have been convinced that it was immoral and would have discussed its immorality under the heading of violations of the virtues of prudence or poverty. Yet justice has traditionally been the virtue which enables us to give to each what he properly deserves. The use of time and energy in a world where both are in short supply requires more, I think, than the tradition of prudence to direct us. Justice imposes a sense of *reality* on us; it is a hard-nosed demanding virtue. I chose to use "justice" as a heading for a consideration of the proper regulation of such matters as our career and our finances precisely because both of these issues are far more demanding in our society than they were in the past. The same sober restraint which the Romans manifested in their sense of justice, we must manifest in our use of the ordering of our time and finances.

Our career and our income are but two of the worst manifestations of how beleaguered and battered our sense of "justice" really is, but there are other insistent demands swirling about us; our clients and our employers will demand every second of our time if we give them the opportunity. Unless we have the courage and the self-confidence to draw a line and say that there are some things that no corporate organization or no client may legitimately demand of us, then we will become their slaves. As one M.D. put it, rather graphically, "All my clients are enemies. If I give them a chance, they will destroy me." It might be remarked, however, that the socialization of the medical student, intern, and resident is such that most doctors don't believe that they are really competent and dedicated members of their profession unless they let every other responsibility in their lives fade away in the face of the insistent demands of the great god Medicine. The doctor who proudly states how many hours each week he has put into his practice and how little time he has for anything else is certain that he is thus stating his excellence as a doctor and is quite unconscious that he is also exposing his poverty as a human being. The whole insane ritual of sacrifice of time in human relationships demanded of the intern and the resident is part of the medical myth and probably notably impedes progress in health services. But, given the fact that the high priests of the medical profession are committed to the idea that the worth of the profession is measured (a.) by level of income, and (b.) by the commitment of time demanded of its members, we are unlikely to have much reform.

There are also the insistent demands of raising our children. Child rearing is not a joy, or a delight, or a challenge; it is a project. We must agonize over which schools they are to be sent to, what kinds of teachers they have, what their relationships are with their teachers, how they are doing in comparison with others, what their "social adjustment" is like, whether they have had all the proper inoculations, and whether they are getting the literary, artistic, and cultural experiences that are demanded of people with our state in life.

Passionate concern with the rearing and education of children is highly useful, since it can be an excellent substitute for love. If we are really afraid to respect our children as individual human beings with personhoods of their own, if we're really afraid to trust them, if we're really afraid to assure them constantly of their own worth and value, then obsessiveness about Boy Scout troop activities or the teacher's remarks at our monthly, awkward confrontation with her, or progress in piano lessons are excellent substitutes. Furthermore, such concerns also provide us with magnificent excuses. If something goes wrong in the child's life, the real problem then can be traced back to the second-grade teacher who didn't really teach Johnny how to read.

I am particularly amused by the cult of various special forms of education. The snobbery which, for example, surrounds the Montessori schools is hardly justified by any of the empirical research done on the effectiveness of these schools; but such snobbery still provides parents with an opportunity of feeling that they are really doing the "right thing" for their children. It is not only depressing, it is also baloney.

The unpleasant truth about education is that it really doesn't make much difference what kind of school you send your child to. Most education, be it of a very elite private type or the very average public type, has only marginal impact on the children who participate in it. One might say that all education is equally good or all education is equally bad; I personally would incline to the latter. But, nevertheless, the best predictor of a child's performance in school is not the training of the teacher and the number of students in the classroom, or the educational methods used, but (the correlation coefficients with the variables are slight and almost nonexistent) the child's intelligence and the scholarly atmosphere in the home from which he comes. If all the time and the energy and effort expended on worrying about what goes on in the school were replaced by parental effort to become a better-educated person, the impact on the intellectual growth of the child would be immense. But somehow or the other our feelings of insecurity, insufficiency, and guilt won't permit us to do that. We must harass the teacher, examine the schools, worry about the grades; somehow or the other that will help Johnny to be a good student. We really can't believe that a concern about books and ideas in the family atmosphere will help at all.

There are the demands of our social obligations. There are so many people we must have back for dinner, there are so many parties, dinners, and receptions we must make, so many presents we must give, so many Christmas cards we must send, so many people we must telephone, so many old friends that we must see. Social life, that was primarily intended to be enjoyable and recreational, becomes one more mammoth burden. For some people, even the sending of Christmas cards and purchasing of Christmas presents—surely one of the most enjoyable experiences of the whole year—becomes a horrendous experience, one that produces all kinds of fears and guilts, procrastination, and moral paralysis. God help such a person if he ever feels a temptation actually to enjoy his social life; there couldn't be any greater sin.

There are also the demands of our life style. Because of who we are and where we live and what we aspire to be, there are certain organizations we must belong to, certain activities in which we must engage, certain commitments we must make. It may be the Parish Society or the Christian Family Movement, or the League of Women Voters, a professional association, or the Junior League, or a benefit concert, or an underground parish, or a lecture by an expert, or a trip to a circus, or responsibility to the alumni association, or the board of the parents' auxiliary—any or perhaps all of these must be done, they are part of the obligations of our life. We don't do them because we want to do them, we don't do them because we enjoy doing them, we do them because we have to do them, because we are compelled to do them, because if we do not do them we will be empty and worthless.

We need to be over-committed in order to be sure, over-committed to our careers, over-committed to money, over-committed to our children, over-committed to our social obligations, over-committed to our life style. We may be willing to admit in theory that we'll be a better professional if we can relax in our attitudes toward our career, that we can handle money only when money is not a big problem, that "salutatory neglect" is a great thing for children, that if the social life is not fun, it ought to be stopped, and that over-commitment to organizations and projects is compulsive. But even though we admit all these things in theory, there's not much we can do about it, because we don't have enough confidence in ourselves. We are over-committed in order not to take any risks. We may not have to do these things to be esteemed, but we don't want to take the chance that by not doing them we will lose the esteem on which we so much depend. Not having any esteem of ourselves, the esteem of others is crucial for us. It is much better to over-commit ourselves than to take the risk of underestimating the level of commitment that is required. For to choose among our commitments would require decisiveness and decisiveness in its turn requires decisions and decisions, at least effective ones, require that we have confidence in the decision maker. The decision maker is ourself and he's not very good at making decisions so we're not prepared to run the risk.

All of the above is pretty sick: we have more leisure and more affluence than man has ever known, but we're not able to enjoy the affluence or take advantage of the leisure. We spend the money unwisely and do not enjoy the things we have purchased with it. We fill up our leisure with obligations that bring us neither satisfaction nor growth. We resolutely refuse to take control either of our money or our leisure for fear that we're not adequate to cope with these massive realities, and so we become slaves to money and slaves of social obligations and lead lives which are not only joyless, but also unjust.

Therefore, in my sense of the word, a just man is the man *who takes control.* It's difficult to practice this kind of justice. First of all, the just man must make realistic appraisal of himself and of what expectations he can legitimately have for himself. Given the compulsive desires for achievement, inculcated both by his parents and by the larger society, this realistic appraisal of himself is difficult and for many impossible. It involves recognizing both one's strengths and one's weaknesses, what one can expect legitimately to do and what one can permit others legitimately to demand. But even to attempt this sort of assessment requires a confidence in the self that is rare in contemporary society.

Secondly, the just man must put severe limits on the amount of time that he will concede to his career. He must develop a vigorous capacity to say "no" to employer, to clients, to friends, to anyone who wishes to take away the freedom of choice on which control is based.

The just man must systematically search out and eliminate from his life the infertile and non-rewarding uses of time in which he is involved. The time problems come, one suspects, from wasted time; anyone who takes a close look at a professional office will be appalled at the amount of time that is wasted in gossip, in washroom conversations and discussions of football and baseball games, and in lengthy, pointless lunch hours. There are a number of professions and businesses in which only about four hours of the better part of the working day are used for work. A good deal of the time problem results from the non-satisfying, waste of time—a waste that has an almost enervating effect on those who are addicted to it. Similarly, one might wonder how much of the time bind in which the housewife claims to be caught is in fact the result of interminable coffee klatches and of even more interminable telephone conversations. When the woman claims that she has no time for anything, the most revealing response (though hardly the one most likely to win the responder friends) is to ask her how much time each day she spends on the telephone.

The waste of time is a flight from reality, the presumed ugly reality of the trap in which one is caught and the equally ugly reality of one's own failure and incompetence. Only the man who is almost arrogant about his own worth need not escape from reality in fruitless and futile time wastage. The business lunch, the coffee klatch, the washroom conversation, the lengthy phone call to mother are all ways of killing the pain, the pain caused by one's feeling of frustration and worthlessness.

The just man must also assert a rational control over his use of money, a control which is not minute and which does not take freedom and spontaneity out of his spending, but rather, builds the freedom and spontaneity into a rationally planned system. Many married couples are going to need psychotherapy to be able to handle their financial problems *regardless* of how much money they make. For only through protracted counseling are these couples going to be able to face the absurdity of a situation in which their life is dominated by money, despite the fact that they live in a society where there is a superabundance of money.

It is also necessary that we understand and cope with the "compensatory" function of spending. Just as some people eat too much when they feel lonely or rejected, others of us are in-clined to "buy something" when we are discouraged or dis-heartened. Within certain limits, this compensatory function is healthy and positive; the discouraged woman who knows that a new dress or even a new hair style will boost her morale is very wise if she permits herself such an emotional shot in the arm and even wiser if she has worked into her budget oppor-tunities for such compensations. Unfortunately, compulsive buy-ing readily exceeds rational limits. Vicious cycles begin to be generated in which we feel discouraged because of our financial problems, and to get over the discouragement, we buy some-thing to improve our morale and thus make the financial prob-lems even worse. In families inflicted with this problem, denial mechanisms can be very strong; husband, wife, and children can all live a life style far beyond their means by resolutely refusing to face the fact that the life style is totally unrealistic.

Finally, a man who wishes to exercise control must be deter-mined that he is going to enjoy the good things he has; justice and temperance are therefore closely related to one another, and he who is incapable of enjoying that which is his is both intemperate and unjust, and his name is Legion.

I remember several summers ago it became necessary to purchase a new television set to replace the battered old Sony which had served me well for a decade or so. I made the alarming discovery that for an extra one hundred dollars I could present myself with a color television that would enable me to indulge in one of my favorite secret vices—watching professional football games—in fully living color. I have too much pride to go into any great detail about the fantastic emotional and in-tellectual contortions I went through trying to justify and then unjustify the extra expense. The process was made more difficult because I was in one of my late summer pessimistic moods at the time and was fully aware that I might be buying a color TV as a compensatory mechanism. Now, through all of this madness, let me insist, I had really every intention of buying the RCA color TV set which even now I gaze upon fondly across my room; but because of some weird hang-up out of my past, I was not able to do so without inflicting a certain amount of punishment upon myself in the process, a punishment which I might say was enhanced by the fact that the Chicago Bears had an utterly disastrous season that year; but then most every year is disastrous for the Bears.

There are no easy rules which everyone can apply to the question of whether they should buy a color television set, join the League of Women Voters, work after supper tonight, call Johnny's teacher, or finally clean out that hall closet. The illusion that textbooks can provide answers was never a very healthy one, but it is clearly quite worthless in the modern world. How each one of us is to establish control over his varying obligations is, in the final analysis, something each one has to decide for himself. Though in the context of understanding what the forces and pressures are which make for a lack of control, we can only give ourselves to others in love and affection when we have established some kind of secure and rational control over the obligations of our lives. If we are giving ourselves to others because of obligations, then the gift is a forced, half-hearted, and incomplete one. The man who has not balanced and controlled his obligations is not a free man and he is not a just man, he is not capable of rendering to the multitude of Caesars who surround him those things which are Caesar's and hence he is also incapable of rendering to God the things that are God's.

6. *OK, Louis, Put Down That Plow*
(FORTITUDE)

The negative image of temperance is the blue-nosed prude. The negative image of justice is the stern, cold judge and the negative image of fortitude is the martyr throwing herself into the flames before the Roman soldier can push her. I suspect that the martyr was really a coward; she was afraid that if she waited another second she would have lost her nerve. Just as the other side of the coin of the prude is the libertine and of the calculating judge is the hardened criminal, so the other side of someone who eagerly seeks out suffering and death is a fearful, cowering weakling who will do anything, just anything, in order that he might be left alone. For a modern image of fortitude, I would be inclined to choose Vince Lombardi refusing to settle for a tie against the Dallas Cowboys in the last seconds of a championship game. The brave man is not the foolish man, not the man who's eager to suffer, but rather, the confident man who knows what he can do and what he can't do. The secret to Coach Lombardi's fantastic success with the Green Bay Packers is that he knew better than any of his players what they could do, and most, if not all of them, could do far more than they were willing to admit to themselves.

In the last chapter, we noted that justice was taught to us in both irrelevant and falsely specific ways. We didn't spend nearly as much time on fortitude as we did on justice, but still what we got out of our consideration of the subject was surely ludicrous. The brave man was he who defended his faith against the agnostic professor in a secular university, or the zealous proselytizer who argued religion with the one who was unfortunate enough to sit next to him in an airplane, or the austere believer who resolutely refused to eat meat on Friday even though nothing else was available, or the village convert maker who kept a list of the number of bemused Protestants that he dragged to the rectory basement for inquiry classes, or the missionary who left the ease of home and family to be a modern St. Francis Xavier in such uncivilized places as Tokyo or Hong Kong or Manila or Rio or Santiago.

But the secular university faculties are probably more kind to Catholicism than are the faculties at Catholic universities. We can eat meat on Friday now until our heart's content. In the ecumenical age, convert making, such as it is, is necessarily more permissive and soft-sell. We've come to understand that one need not go very far from home to be a missionary; indeed, Harvey Cox has even assured us that the suburbs can be mission fields.

So fortitude has been transformed; it no longer need involve physical courage or that kind of militant gall which Jews describe so beautifully as *chutzpa*. It is now, rather, the courage to be—which; if the truth be told, is a far more difficult courage than that specified by the older image of fortitude. The new model of fortitude is not the Roman maiden throwing herself into the fire, but rather Thomas More carefully and cautiously playing out the string, refusing to be precipitate, but also refusing to yield one bit of his own integrity. The courage More displayed did not consist in defending his faith, but in refusing to lose his cool. All of us must die sometime. More demonstrated how brave men die, not needlessly, not foolishly, but rather as they lived—with complete confidence in their own faith and their own goodness.

But if we have come to see fortitude in a different light, we must admit that the new light seems to make it a more obscure virtue. The face of the enemy has changed. He is no longer that mean old agnostic professor, or the wild savage with a spear in his hand, or the cruel Roman centurion; in fact he doesn't have a face at all, or if he does, it is rather astonishing that it looks much like our own. In the old image of fortitude, the fears we were supposed to face were all precisely specified and accurately named, but now the fears which we must face are not so much on the outside as on the inside of the self and they have no names. Maybe there are those on the outside who are telling us that we should not have the Courage to Be, but they are not very important. The real enemy is the voice within that warns us of the risk and the foolishness of trying to have the Courage to Be.

The situation of contemporary man is paradoxical. He's far more sophisticated about himself and he has far more technological aids to enhance his personal freedom than did any of his predecessors. He also has more time and more self-knowledge for love, but also more time for fear, loneliness, and anxiety. Love may be more accessible but it is also more necessary. Man may be more free but he is also more easy to manipulate. Meaningfulness has escalated; what would have passed as a meaningful relationship but a generation ago is now viewed as unsatisfactory. A posture vis-à-vis the world which a generation ago would have been thought to be quite tolerable would now be thought of as unbearably lonely. It has been a peculiar kind of revolution, in which man's expectations about himself and his own capacities have increased even more rapidly than has his knowledge about how to cope with himself. Modern man sees both himself and the world as more complex and more difficult to satisfy than his parents would have believed possible. We have more than we've ever had before but we want far more, and in its absence we feel frustrated and anxious.

It was easier in another society and in another time to stay walled up within ourselves. We could repress our longings for fulfillment more easily when we didn't know that any alternatives were possible and when there were not others around us preaching insistently that there were options to fear and loneliness. Loneliness becomes intolerable only when there is no hope for breaking out of it. When hope appears and we are faced with the awesome necessity of responding to it, the problem becomes acute; we do permit a little trust, a little self-disclosure, a little bit of love, a little bit of pleasure into our lives. Then we realize, not just theoretically, but with a sharp pang that transfixes our whole personality, that alternatives are possible, but alternatives for which we will have to pay a heavy price. It is the payment of that price which requires fortitude.

Self-hatred and self-rejection are not pleasant to contemplate but there is a certain consoling and comforting complacency about them because they excuse us from effort, excuse us from trying, excuse us from exposing ourselves to the inspection of others; if we are convinced that we are ugly and worthless, then we at least know the nature of the agony with which we are dealing; we become familiar with it, attached to it, and afraid to give it up. The new pain of breaking out of the self-loathing is frightening. We agree with the old Irish saying, "Better the devil you know than the devil you don't know." It has been comfortable not growing and growth is likely to be very uncomfortable; fixation is stable and certain, growth is irregular, erratic, and unpredictable; it takes time and we're not sure how much time, nor do we know what it will be like at any one point in time. When the world says to us, now you can grow, it is in fact asking us to buy the proverbial pig in the poke; we're not sure we like the pig and we're not impressed by the poke.

So it takes courage to make the plunge necessary to begin growth. It takes courage, further, to accept the evidence of respect and admiration that are to be observed all around us. It has always seemed to me as one who has counseled the young that the most difficult part of the task is to persuade them that I am not kidding them, or not going through some kind of social scientific act, or not working an experiment on them when I assure them that they have immense value and worth. I really don't know that I've yet been successful in persuading anybody that he underestimates himself. I know many beautiful women who have gone through life thus far convinced that they are ugly, despite overwhelming evidence to the contrary. I know many men with great sensitivity and insight who are persuaded that they are quite insensitive and that the only contribution that they have to make to society is that they are tough organizers. I know many men and women with first-rate intelligences and considerable literary competence who believe that they have nothing worth putting down on paper, even to the extent that they will deliberately sabotage their own literary style lest they be awakened with the shock that they have said something worthwhile. I know many young men and women who are admired by everyone they know and yet who are convinced that they are disliked and rejected.

Their parents have done a marvelous job on all of these people to damage their morale and blight their self-esteem so that they cannot see the obvious. They are very good at making comparisons with others, comparisons which are always unfavorable to themselves. Of course, the comparisons are either completely inaccurate or are based on highly selective criteria on which they are bound to lose.

The brilliant lawyer does not trust his intellect because he has read no philosophy or theology books (and, of course, is not about to try to read them), and the young woman with marvelous insight into human behavior argues that she does not want to accept these insights because she lacks liberal arts training, and the slender woman whose sexual elegance disconcerts any man who looks at her feels honestly that she is unattractive because her measurements are not quite those of Miss America. The charismatic personality who can kindle enthusiasm in thirty seconds feels diffident because he or she lacks confidence to be able to be "responsible" to those in whom the enthusiasm has been stirred. The woman who can charm people into co-operation feels the need to intimidate them because she doubts her own charm; the man whose insights are valued by all his friends keeps the insights to himself because he never gets any reaction to them, at least any reaction that he will permit himself to see, though everyone else sees it.

The capacity for self-deception about one's own impact on others is virtually limitless and it takes immense courage to believe that others speak the truth when they assert that you do have such an impact.

It takes courage, though perhaps not quite so much, to tell others how important they are and how much they mean. It takes courage to offer friendship to others, it takes courage to begin to disclose ourselves to them, it takes courage to speak our ideas even though we are not sure of them, it takes courage to be skeptical about our own masks and defense mechanisms, it takes courage to question our own complacent certainties about ourselves and others, it takes courage to ask for help and even more courage to accept the help when it is offered, it takes courage to admit that it's not too late to grow, it takes courage to say no when our dignity or our privacy or our freedom are being violated, it takes courage, as we shall remark in the next chapter, to take calculated risks that are both risky and calculated, it takes courage to say yes when someone offers us love, it takes courage to finish the things that we have started, because when they are finished they stand for all to see as a public manifestation of our competency and our worth. But without courage faith doesn't mean much, our hope is weak, and our love is chained down. The brave man is happy; the coward is sad—but we much prefer sadness to the risk implied by happiness.

And the trouble with courage is that there's never enough of it. If we could only be courageous for a day or a week or a month or a year and then be able to put it aside, all would be well, but we know that if we once start to be courageous there's never going to be any stop to it. If you once start taking risks, then you're going to spend the rest of your life taking risks. Sometimes it seems unfair that the Lord has given us the alternative that he has: either the dull pain of complacent and narrow self-rejection or the disturbing uncertainty of courageous self-affirmation. It would have been so nice if there had been a middle ground.

The courageous man is a gambler, not a reckless gambler who takes chances purely for the sake of taking chances, but a gambler who plays to win. He takes chances only when the chances are necessary for victory and only when he has very carefully calculated which chance is the most appropriate. But having performed his calculations and having determined that the risk is necessary, he takes it. He knows that the only way to be sure of not losing is not to play, and not to play is dull and frustrating, so he plays and he plays to win. In the words of Vincent Lombardi, "Winning isn't everything, it's the only thing."

But the problem is that to be able to win, to be able to take the gambles necessary for winning, he must first be free to win. He must put aside the foolish fears of inadequacy which tell him that he cannot win and that it is foolish to try. The man who believes that it is foolish to try is not free to try; he lacks the courage to be, because he also lacks the courage to believe. He wouldn't do on the Green Bay Packers, nor does he do in the Christian Church.

One of our great fears is the fear of disapproval or of more disapproval than we perceive aimed at us presently. This particular fear, like so many others, is absorbed from our early family backgrounds, where the most horrendous thing that could happen would be to have our parents disapprove of us. Unfortunately most of us were unable to work out our relationships with our parents in such a way that we could value their approval without being totally dependent upon it. Hence every parent figure that comes along is a potential source of great fear, whether it be a religious superior or bishop or monsignor, or a senior partner or an employer, or a teacher, or a spouse, or even the director of the National Opinion Research Center.* The

---

* I kicked this fear before I kicked the fear of monsignors. Indeed, I stopped being afraid of bishops, archbishops, and even cardinals before I stopped being afraid of monsignors.

parent figure is perceived as having power which will be focused on our destruction if he disapproves of us. Therefore it is necessary to do all that we can to win his approval. In the meantime we begin to hate and resent him because of his power and seek out ways to punish and frustrate him. It's all very neat, particularly if the power figure himself, or herself, actually has the need to play a parental role. If he doesn't, then it's rather tough on him, because he's going to be a parent whether he wants to or not. This may blight friendship or the possibility of mutuality, but its much better than risking the courage required to recognize that the power figure can become a colleague. Implicit in such a recognition, of course, is the realization that we too are capable of being power figures.

The fear of disapproval coupled with the desire to punish the disapproving parent produces particularly messy results in a marriage, especially if, as happens all too frequently, both spouses happen to have married parent figures: the wife desperately needs her husband's approval; the husband desperately needs his wife's approval, but neither is willing to give approval, because withholding approval is a form of punishment which enables one to get back at the disapproving parent figure. The marriage, therefore, is immersed in timidity, fear, and cowardice —sometimes to such an extent that courage on the part of one member or another is likely to do more harm than good. The two spouses will have to become brave simultaneously for anything to develop.

Approval and encouragement in any friendship relation are terribly important, because even at our best we are unsure of ourselves in any intimate relationship and especially in the powerful and indeed overwhelming intimacy of marriage. While approval is important, however, it cannot be permitted to become all-important. On the contrary, we are only able to enter a relationship that has a chance of success if we approve of ourself sufficiently so that the other's approval, while welcome and reassuring, is not absolutely essential. In friendship we are principally concerned with giving, revealing, and reassuring the other, but if these goals are pre-empted by our need to attain reassurance back, then the friendship is rooted in weakness and timidity and is doomed before it starts.

Parent figures as long as they remain parent figures cannot be good friends. The parent-child relationship before the child becomes an adult is essentially a dependency relationship; the child depends upon his parent for his food, his clothes, his housing, and for his emotional well-being. It is the parent's role to reassure and the child's role to be reassured. The relationship is a useful and indeed marvelous one but it is not adult friendship. On the contrary, in some respects it is the opposite of adult friendship, since it is the role of the child to be reassured and the role of the adult friend to give himself in reassurance. Marriage to a parent figure may function at some low level of effectiveness if the dependent person is willing to spend the rest of his life playing the role of the child or if it is impossible for the dependent person to be anything else but a child. Some kinds of personal intimacy can be rooted in a parent-child relationship, so long as the child figure is incapable or unwilling to grow up and so long as the parent figure is incapable or unwilling to accept mutuality. But both the marriage and the adult friendship that are based on the parent-child model are based on mutual weaknesses, the weakness of a child who needs a parent and the weakness of an adult who would prefer a child to another adult. While such relationships are in some sense cowardly, they can be very stable and even satisfying, though not nearly so satisfying as a relationship between two adults, both moderately endowed with courage.

One wonders whether the sexual dimension in parent-child marriage can ever be very satisfying, since it would seem that a ceiling had been put on its possibilities for development. It may seem unduly harsh to call such relationships incestuous but we must call them cowardly. If you can only enjoy sex with someone who is psychologically your child, it suggests that you might really be afraid of an adult. If you are able only to respond sexually to a powerful and reassuring figure who neither needs nor wants you to be an adult, then you presumably do not have much self-respect. Both the parent and the child in such a relationship are very incomplete, adolescent, childish personalities and their marriage is a child marriage. There is not likely to be much experimentation, much novelty, much excitement, much challenge, or much growth.

But one of the advantages of the parent-child relationship, either in friendship or marriage, is that the demands and the responsibilities are fairly clearly stated. The coward is afraid of demands and responsibilities. In his perspective, responsibility is something which proves your worth and value. A demand is something to which you must respond or else your dignity and value will be denied. All obligations, all responsibility, and all demands are terribly threatening.

Because there is so much terrifying emotional investment in responding to a demand, the coward flees responsibilities either by pretending they're not there or by making them so difficult that he can refuse to respond to them on the grounds of in-adequacy and incompetency. The plea for sympathy because of one's worthlessness is a marvelous escape from responsibility.

What the coward is unable to understand is that there are demands and responsibilities which can be made and indeed which must be made by those who love us and whose love is going to be completely unaffected by whether we respond or not. Parent figures may have taught us that if we fail to respond, we are worthless and condemned. But lovers love us just as much even when we are irresponsible, although our irresponsibility may hurt them. Thus a husband may legitimately demand that his wife, with his assistance, keep their house presentable and orderly, though not compulsively neat. She will, in all likelihood, see this demand as something that questions her very value as a human being and respond to it by appealing for compassion and sympathy because of her inability to respond to the demand. After a while, her husband learns that the demand is dys-functional to the marriage relationship and settles down to make the best of a messy house. If the wife could only perceive that his demand has nothing to do with her worth, but simply is a functional requirement for a satisfactory friendship, then the responsibility would be seen as minor and not horrendous, something to which she could respond with great ease. However, the insecure and self-rejecting person cannot understand the concept of minor responsibilities; either a responsibility is major and must be imposed with powerful sanction by an outside agent or it is nonexistent. Neither can the cowardly, self-rejecting person cope with the concept of a responsibility to disclose his own talents. If one has the ability to write or to sing, for example, this ability becomes a responsibility, but not a responsibility that outside agents impose in order that we may pass a test to establish our own value. Rather, it is a responsibility that ought to flow joyously from our own inner self-esteem and self-respect. However, the coward rejects this kind of responsibility. If anything is an obligation, it is an externally imposed obligation that is aimed at testing our worth and as such must be feared and hated.

In the marriage union, the demand for sexual responsiveness can take on terrifying importance and result in great anguish for both partners. One spouse perceives the other as demanding a more intense sexual response; if the first partner valued his (or her) own sexuality, this demand would be seen as valid and challenging, and also as offering an opportunity for great pleasure and fulfillment. But if the first partner has grave doubts about his (or her) sexual attractiveness, then the demand is seen as a fearsome obligation to which one is completely incapable of responding. So instead of attempting a response, the inadequate spouse actually lowers the level of effort and appeals rather for sympathy and compassion and understanding because of his (or her) sexual inadequacy. The other spouse catches on quickly, though he perhaps does not realize that he is being subtly punished for making what his partner considers intolerable demands. He has not been able to establish, because the other does not want to believe him, that he seeks increased sexual intensity not as a proof of love but as a greater fulfillment of a love about which he has no doubt. Therefore, because he has been tricked by the plea for compassion, the rejected spouse gradually withdraws his demand and is content with a level of married love which may be real enough but is still limited and inadequate.

It is a classic case of the lack of courage on both sides. The "sexually inadequate" spouse does not have the courage to believe in his immense sexual attractiveness, he cannot believe that his physical presence has seduced his partner into more intense desire, and so, because of fear and low self-esteem, he turns aside the partner's love. The partner, on the other hand, does not have the courage to persist gently and subtly break through the barriers of uncertainty and self-rejection and persuade his beloved that the attractiveness he perceives is overwhelming. Neither partner has the courage to discuss the problem honestly and openly. Cowardice has blighted, if not destroyed, the marriage friendship.

An intimate relationship between two adults requires some risky learning experiences: bravery and communication and sensitivity to the other person. Unless our parents were skillful in relating to each other as adult friends, then we do not have readily available models of this kind of behavior. The learning experience may be painful, particularly because in the process we are forced to make the alarming though ultimately marvelous discovery that we can respond to a demand. We can assume responsibilities not because we have to, not because our worth depends upon it, but because we want to and because we love the person to whom we are responding.

It also takes courage to fulfill commitments, because commitments become responsibilities. If we are still hung up on parent figures, then responsibilities are things that we must fulfill to demonstrate our own worth. Since we are not confident of our own worth, we become, in a marvelously self-fulfilling prophecy, incompetent at exercising commitments. If something is finished, it's out there for people to look at as a manifestation of ourselves. They will judge it and judge us by it. Rather than run the risk of being judged incompetent after we've done something, it is much better to hold back, to persuade ourselves that we will do it someday and put off the terrible day of judgment, when it will be finished and we will be judged by it. Far better to be thought a procrastinator than a failure. Of course, as long as the task is incomplete, the parent figure, who is seen as demanding completion, can be controlled and punished by its incompleteness.

One of the classic examples of this lack of Courage to Be Finished is a doctoral dissertation. In almost every circumstance, graduate school faculties view dissertations as merely academic exercises and not as works that have to have a mark of genius. They are only too eager for students to finish their dissertations because a large list of "ABDs"* is a very negative judgment on a department. In many instances indeed, the department would do almost anything to get rid of an "ABD"—up to the point of writing the dissertation for him.

But the student knows better. He knows there are all sorts of traps and tricks set for him, he knows that the faculty is out to get him, he knows the faculty has power and they disapprove of him, he knows that the degree is terribly important. His worth depends upon it and therefore, of course, it must be a horrendously difficult task. He must torment himself and he must procrastinate in every way possible to avoid the ultimate moment of truth, when he must sit across the table from his parent-enemies of the department and have them sit in judgment on his worth. If he only realized that all the examining board wants to do is to finish the exam so that they can get back to read the latest issue of the *New York Review of Books,* he would be first horrified and then disappointed. How can something that is so important to him be so unimportant to them? So he drags the dissertation on, protecting himself against judgment and punishing his advisors for making such insensible demands upon him. He is a coward and may even cheerfully admit that he is a coward; indeed, he may admit it

* "All but Dissertation."

for years of therapy to his analyst, but he's still not going to take the chance of finishing that dissertation.*

Through most of this chapter, I have described the difficulties, the agony, the torment of the Courage to Be, and the Courage to Be an Adult. But there is another side to the coin. Courage may be confusing, it is also exhilarating; courage may be painful, but it is also exciting and challenging. Risking victory in order that one might achieve victory is great fun—if you don't believe it, ask Vince Lombardi, Bart Starr, and Jerry Kramer. We can choose to be little men or big men. If we are little men, we may reassure ourselves for our littleness by snipping at big men and by trying to cut them down to size. Even at best, such an enterprise quickly becomes dull and uninteresting. Or we can choose to be big men; others will snipe at us and we will make mistakes and sometimes we'll fall flat on our faces and sometimes we'll fail and sometimes we'll make utter fools of ourselves, but life will never be dull, and at least, on occasion, we will have the exhilarating feeling that we have won, that we are national champs.

*Whatever my other faults are (and as the reader has probably suspected, most of what is written in this book is based on self-analysis), I don't have this one. My dissertation was finished in six weeks.

7. May I Borrow That Computer You Have in Your Pocket?
(PRUDENCE)

In the watered-down version of the Christian spiritual tradition popular before the Vatican Council, prudence, along with obedience, occupied the place of the most important of the virtues. While justice dealt with the moral problems of the past and fortitude, with unrealities in the present, prudence dealt in a highly specific fashion with the realities of the present. It presented to us the guiding principles according to which we were expected to be able to respond to every important decision that we faced. Its basic principle was quite simple; prudence meant doing absolutely *nothing* that *had not* been done before and *everything* that *had* been done before. Fortitude was the Roman martyr throwing herself into the fire. Justice was the blind, insensitive judge, temperance was the sexless prude. And prudence? Well, prudence was a fat Irish monsignor saying "no."

Prudence meant not taking any risks; it meant not offending anybody; it meant not reading magazines because they might have dirty pictures, or not going to the movies during vacation because there might be beautiful women in the movies, even occasionally dressed in ballet costumes*; it meant not reading

* For us it was pronounced "ballot" and took us a while to figure out what we were suppose to avoid.

novels because they would give us bad thoughts; it meant taping up Shakespeare's sonnets in our English texts because we might get homosexual ideas from such sonnets; it meant not risking relationships with people because we might get involved with them and thus lose our vocation; it meant staying aloof, being distant and reserved because if we took a single chance on intimacy, that might be the bullet that had our name on it. Prudence meant not doing anything unless we were told by our superior to do it, and even then it was probably best if we asked our superior for advice on how he wanted us to do it. Prudence was not, as St. Thomas Aquinas thought, a virtue which inclined us to behavior appropriate to the circumstances we were in; it was, rather, a virtue which inclined us to do as little as humanly possible and preferably absolutely nothing.

Such a view of prudence was essentially protectionist, rooted in the defensive mentality of the Counter-Reformation Church and reinforced by the defensive mentality of immigrant American Catholicism. In the seminary we got an especially strong dose of it, but it was not exactly absent from the rest of American Catholic culture either. Prudence dictated that we stay away from non-Catholic schools lest we lose our faith at such schools—and a weak faith it must have been to be so easily lost. (Available statistical data say that most people don't lose their faith at non-Catholic schools, but that's another matter.)

Prudence meant further that we avoid mixed marriages because those "damned mixed marriages," as the Irish monsignori called them, led to a loss of faith. (The data here show that holding constant the religious background from which a person comes, mixed marriages have no impact on religious behavior. The relationship between a low level of religious practice and mixed marriage is a function of the fact that those who are not very religious are more likely to enter mixed marriage, but the marriage itself is more of an effect than a cause.) Prudence warned us that we should hold ourselves back from the non-Catholic culture and become a subculture or "open ghetto" where we could preserve our values (particularly our values on birth control) from being corrupted by the rest of American society. Prudence told us not to take chances; departing very far from the rectory and the parochial school was, by definition, a chance.

No one is fated by his environment to lose anything; compulsive and superstitious fear of environments suggests that there was a very weak faith to begin with; it also suggests that those Christians who so desperately needed the protection that prudence demanded for them were hardly to be trusted as being heralds of the good news. For the good news seemed to make them weak rather than strong.

It is appropriate, therefore, to return to St. Thomas' notion of prudence: it's a virtue which enables us to do the right thing at the right time. To put the matter in more modern terms, prudence is a virtue which aids us in the difficult art of decision making. It's not an a priori virtue, its answers cannot be obtained from a theology manual, or from a set of rules and constitutions, or from the wise advice of a spiritual director. It is, rather, an empirical, problematic virtue. It helps us make decisions in a world of obscurity and grayness.

Prudence is not a virtue which will guarantee us that we will avoid mistakes. On the contrary, it's far more likely to guarantee us that we *will* make mistakes. There are not many certainties in the human condition. Most of the decisions we make in our lives (beside the basic commitments of faith) would best be based on a high degree of probability.

Working as we do with ambiguities and probabilities, we must have enough self-confidence, enough flexibility to run the risk of making mistakes and then living with them if needs be, for we learn from mistakes. John Kennedy learned from the Bay of Pigs disaster not to trust the military and hence learned how to handle the far more serious missile crisis. Lyndon Johnson apparently did not learn from his mistakes and continued to trust the advice of the military until it brought him down to disaster in Vietnam. Only a man who is ready to admit his mistakes can learn from them, only a man who has enough confidence in himself will run the risk of mistakes and then honestly face them when he has to.

We will not be damned, save by superficial critics, for making mistakes, but we will be damned if we refuse to learn from our mistakes or, even worse, refuse to run the risk of mistakes. Prudence and fortitude are closely linked. Prudence helps us to weigh the probability, measure the ambiguities, calculate the grayness. Then fortitude tells us, despite the fact that we're not absolutely positive, it is still clear that we must act, and therefore we will act.

One of the oddities in contemporary life is that the environment pretends to us that there is little room for mistakes, but actually there is a great deal of room. We try to persuade young people that they must make their career decisions early in high school, but in truth, they can make them any time in their late twenties without suffering much in the way of handicap. We attempt to make them believe that a failure in high school or in college is a blot on their record which will never be erased, but actually the system, more or less reluctantly, permits people to have many failures. We attempt to convince the young professional that the slightest mistake in the early part of his career will blight the rest of the career, but actually the demand for professional talent is so great that the system is willing to tolerate many, many mistakes and not merely from young men, either.

If we are in the business of working with people and particularly if we are priests or religious, we are urged to believe that one mistake may lead to someone's eternal damnation, a notion based on the obviously heretical assumption that one person can damn another person. We are also warned that if we step out of line and do something original, particularly if it should fail, it will be held against us and people will remember us as an unsuccessful innovator; but there are so many unsuccessful innovations that these are promptly forgotten and the successful innovator is the one that everybody remembers. We are told that when we make mistakes we must use maximum energy to justify ourself, to protect our public image, but it is the weak man who seeks to justify himself and also an uninformed man, because most people are not interested and will not listen to our justifications. While we waste our time vainly trying to cover over our mistake, we miss the opportunity to learn from it.

Yet it is tempting to be indecisive. The indecisive man—the man who refuses to make decisions, who procrastinates on decisions until they're no longer necessary, or who makes them and then quickly withdraws them in the face of opposition—this man is indeed preserved from making a fool out of himself, unless you happen to think it is real foolishness to hide yourself behind timidity and indecisiveness.

The indecisive man, that is to say, the imprudent man, is the first cousin of the coward we discussed in the last chapter. He does not accept himself or the good news, he does not believe strongly enough in his life project to be able to focus his energies, even to the point of making a decision. When someone comes up to him and eagerly asks whether the good news is true, the indecisive man scratches his head in puzzlement and says, "Well, I'm not sure but I think it might be." He is afraid to be cold and not brave enough to be hot; so he fluctuates around various temperatures of lukewarmness, despite the rather unpleasant fate predicted for the lukewarm. He knows his life project is important, he knows that it will drift if he does not make decisions about it, he knows that if he chooses to go North he most assuredly cannot go South, but maybe it's a mistake to go North, maybe he should go South. He does not go anywhere, which of course avoids mistakes and it also avoids movement.

The free man, on the other hand, is the one who enjoys the ability to choose between alternatives, an ability which is not merely theoretical, but practical. He actually can choose one alternative or the other. He can realistically face the implications of all the advantages he is going to give up by not traveling South, but on balance he decides that it is still better to travel North, because north is the direction more appropriate to his talents and interests and also one that he thinks he will enjoy more. He knows that he will miss things in the South and there will be things in the North he won't like, but he is also confident enough of himself to know that no matter how bad things may get in the North he will still be able to make the best of them. He knows that he will be happy in the North, he also knows that he will not trouble himself by asking whether he would be happier if he had gone South, because such questions deal with an unreal world that never existed. He does not choose the northern journey lightly or impulsively or at the last minute, he weighs the alternatives carefully, calculates the probabilities, consults with the wisest of men, and listens very carefully to his own instincts. He is not terribly surprised that the final decision that he makes is the one that his most inner self was inclined to in the first place, but still he is prudently cautious about those instincts; while they're usually right, it is still discreet to check them out against the judgments of reason and the judgment of other men's instincts.

The prudent man, the free man, the decisive man does not agonize, for example, over the choice of a spouse. He permits himself no illusions about the weaknesses of his beloved, but he also makes certain he knows her strengths. He knows that his marriage, like all marriages, is problematic, that there will be good moments in it, even ecstatic ones, but also that there will be difficulties and tensions which will have to be patiently and cautiously worked out. If his beloved is not perfect, neither is he; but he is confident enough of himself to know that, despite the difficulties and tensions he will encounter together with his spouse, he and she will be able to find happiness. He does not seek basic happiness in marriage, but rather, an increased fulfillment of happiness. He makes his decision, not indeed with certainty, for no man can have certainty about such a decision, but with confidence. He knows that in some other world, perhaps, he could find another woman who would be a more ideal mate than the one that he has chosen and has chosen him, but he also knows that in the world in which he lives there are many thousands of women with whom he could be happy and who could be happy with him. There may be even others he has not yet met who are better suited than his present beloved, but she and he are suitable enough. What counts is not that perfect matching takes place (and here the computers are probably better than human beings) but that there be patience, kindness, wit, concern, and confidence, and that the two married lovers reinforce each other as they work out the thousands of challenges that they must face in the course of their marriage; at this, computers are no good at all.

The Christian has even less excuse for imprudence than the ordinary man. He believes in a promise that transcends his mistakes. He believes in an evolutionary progress toward the fulfillment of the promise. He believes in the good news. He believes in man's ability to transcend himself and his own limitations, and therefore he ought to have greater confidence and stability in the making of decisions. He attaches greater importance to his life project because he realized that it's a part, however small, of the preparation for the fulfillment of the resurrection promise. He knows that his contribution to the ordering and redeeming of the world is in its own way critical, but he also realizes that his talents are multiform enough that he can make any one of many useful and important contributions.

He is not afraid to participate in anything—as are so many young Americans today—because he does not demand perfect satisfaction from his participation or complete success in it. He knows, rather, that the participation or complete success in it. He knows, rather, that the participation to which he commits himself through his life project may only be moderately successful and only moderately rewarding; like the decisive man, he is willing to settle for moderate success and moderate reward as an alternative to drift and indecision.

He also realizes that there are great successes and great rewards involved in the promise of resurrection. The Christian might want to argue that he has even more reason to be indecisive, because he knows that there is more involved in his decisions; but in fact he ought to realize that he has much less reason to be indecisive, because he is not making the decision by himself and he is not participating in a meaningless process.

How then do we become prudent? Perhaps the first thing to do is to become skillful at listening, listening to our own emotions and listening to the judgments of others. By listening, I do not mean hearing merely the words or the initial response, but rather the penetrating beyond the initial reactions to get at the substance of the response. Our own emotions are so terribly tricky, probably because they are so terribly fearful; our instincts are basically sound but we cannot always be certain whether the response we hear is that of our basic instincts or, rather, of some mask that has gotten in between our perceptions and the depths of our consciousness. Anger, for example, is a marvelous mask; and the angry response delivers a message first to us and then to others, which says, "You have hurt me, I hate you." At a deeper level, however, the response may really mean, "Why don't you love me, or why didn't my parents love me"; at an even deeper level it may mean, "I want to love you."

Sensitivity to our emotions can become convoluted and paralyzing, particularly for those engaged in the early phases of counseling or therapy experiences, but if we are wise and clever and brave, we break through this initial web of confusion and learn to understand our own moods. We know the times when it is very unwise for us to make a decision or to attempt a confrontation. We also know the times when we are so euphoric that we may charge ahead without carefully weighing the risks. We know when our expansiveness and excitement may be dangerous and we also know when our caution and timidity may be dangerous. There is indeed a time to love and a time to hate, a time to laugh and a time to weep, a time to be angry and a time to make peace. The human personality is marvelously complex and the secret of coping with it is not to deny or repress its complexity, but rather, to be in tune to its different manifestations.

In addition to being attuned to our emotions, another help in being a prudent and decisive man is to realize that for most of us the greatest enemy is fear. Fear manifests itself usually as caution or though occasionally excessive as reckless bravado, but it is in either case fear of the weakness and worthlessness of ourselves. We therefore become aware that the most important thing in decision making is to neutralize as best we can the effect of our negative evaluation of ourself.

We must turn, at times when we are uncertain about our capacities to attempt a particular challenge, to the discreet advice of those who know us well, who are most likely to make an accurate and positive judgment about our competencies. We cannot transfer to them the burden of decision making, but we can collect immensely valuable data from them to enable us to have greater confidence in the validity of our decisions.

Another mark of the prudent man is that the time he spends in decision making is appropriate to the circumstances. In most of his decisions, he has enough confidence in his instincts to respond as they dictate without any prolonged agonizing. Unlike the hero in the classic motion picture *Marty,* it does not take him a long period of time to decide what he is going to do tonight or tomorrow night or next week. He reserves for critical decisions or novel decisions the process of long and careful weighing of the facts. The one who has a hard time making a minor decision is almost certain to get completely hung up on the major ones.

The prudent man realizes the importance of what the old spiritual writers called "discerning of spirits." He understands that he is most likely to be best at doing those things which he would be most happy doing. If a decision makes him happy, brings him peace, contentment, and joy in the depths of his personality, then it is the right decision. He knows that in the "discerning of spirits" one has to be constantly aware of the risks of self-deception, but he also learns as he becomes more and more sensitive to his own emotions that the happiness which comes from self-deception is not quite the same thing as the happiness which arises from an open and authentic response of the best of the personality to an alternative that is clearly the better of the ones from which he must choose.

The truly decisive and prudent man eventually reaches that level of self-confidence where he comes to understand that most decisions aren't all that hard and that it is pretty clear in most instances what he should be doing. The obscurity, the confusion, the uncertainty, the hesitation, the doubt generally come not from objective reality but from internal uncertainties, fears, and self-suspicions. It is a quaint paradox that the man who is the most suspicious of himself is also the one who is most likely to deceive himself, and he is also the one most likely to present the most self-confident exterior.

It was frequently said of the late Adlai Stevenson that he was an indecisive, self-anguished man. But I think, rather, that Ambassador Stevenson enjoyed—and quite harmlessly—the act of re-enacting in public the decision making which his quick mind and ready wit accomplished very rapidly in private. Anguish over decisions can be a mask in the Hamlet-like personality but it can also be in other personalities a sign of strength. The Hamlet type really doesn't make his fears known in public, but rather, offers to our view what essentially is a phony decision-making process. It takes truly strong men—and I believe that Ambassador Stevenson was one such man and John Kennedy was another—to acknowledge publicly what are their real doubts and hesitancies. It takes time, of course, to distinguish between the authentic personality who is brave enough to reveal his doubts and the Hamlet who is hiding behind phony anguish. But one need only review the decisions a man makes to find out if he is strong or weak, if he is truly indecisive or merely enjoying explicating the ambiguities of decision making. If Adlai Stevenson was not a Hamlet, and I think he was not, it must still be conceded that the Catholic Church today has many Hamlets in responsible decision-making positions.

But even if I am correct in asserting that for the self-confident man decision making comes rather easy because the realities of a situation generally make the proper decision clear, most of us are not that confident and decision making is still an agony. The virtue of prudence is still a difficult virtue indeed, a far more difficult virtue than we would have believed when we thought it was a virtue which merely inclined us to do nothing.

Decisions are still tough. To make matters worse, the complex, dynamic world in which we live demands of us far more decisions than we ever had to make before. In the Church this was not always the case, because we had a theory which reduced decision making to a minimum. But this theory disappeared before the blast of the strong winds which Pope John unleashed at the Vatican Council. The situation in the Church now is as ambiguous as it is outside and perhaps more so. The need for decisiveness and prudence is likely to increase rather than decrease as the twentieth century jolts forward toward its conclusion. It was so nice when our superiors knew everything and could make our decisions for us; alas, that is a world which will never be again. Come to think of it, it never really was, either.

The more open our relationships are with other human beings, the easier prudence becomes. As we understand them and they understand us, we come to understand ourselves better. In the marvelous interaction of self-revelation and mutual appreciation, we become more firmly grounded in reality and freer of the distorted fantasies that our frightened imagination has generated. A close friendship, a deeply meaningful and happy marriage, a satisfying web of personal relationships are the best guarantees of prudence, because such relationships immerse us in the bright dawn of reality and clear away the fog of self-deception. We see things as they are, because the love of others enables us to see ourselves as we are. We make our decisions, indeed, by ourselves, perhaps in a moment of cold isolation, but we also make them as part of a community, a community whose love and concern for us generates a wisdom that by ourselves we could never attain.

8. *We Had Better Travel Light*
(POVERTY)

Perhaps there is no concept in the Christian spiritual tradition more difficult to reconcile with the modern world than that of poverty. The entire world wages war against poverty, tries to eliminate poverty in the underdeveloped nations, and views poverty as an absolute and unmitigated evil. We may not as yet have acquired quite enough skills to be able to eradicate the roots of poverty; but perhaps by the end of this century we will be able to do so successfully. There is every reason to think, for example, that if the Congress of the United States were willing to spend as much money on the campaign against poverty as it has spent on the war in Vietnam, there would be only small patches of poverty in American society some fifteen years from now.

Yet poverty is an essential element in the Christian spiritual tradition—praised by a long line of spiritual writers, practiced by many saints, and even today urged on those who wish to be followers of Christ in the most perfect possible manner.

One must also say that the worship of poverty, particularly by the lay critics of the clergy (such as Michael Novak, who bemoans the fact that the priests know where the best golf courses and the best restaurants are), is difficult to reconcile with the Christian personalism and humanism that represent the leading edge of Catholic thought today. If the world is good, if mankind is meant to enjoy pleasure, if pleasure opens him up to growth, if it is intended that he be playful, then *why* is deprivation a good thing? At least any more deprivation than is necessary to provide limitations within which he can focus his personality and pursue his life project? I've never seen the satisfactory answer to this question. When it is posed, the worshipers of poverty turn rather pietistically to Charles de Foucault or St. Francis of Assisi as evidence of how important poverty is. Such a style of argumentation has become even more popular today, when the poor have replaced the trade unionist of the past as a social class in which party-line liberals have placed all of their faith.

Part of the problem is that the theories of poverty advanced by religious writers of the past assume a social and economic system that no longer exists. Only after we've faced the change in the economic system, say, from the time of St. Francis of Assisi to the time of John XXIII can we understand the apparent dilemma that the poverty tradition faces and see what implications the tradition really has for the modern world.

First of all, the old theories of poverty assumed a limited and basically inadequate supply of wealth. There were simply not enough material things to go around. If one man had much, it necessarily meant that other men had little, indeed that other men lived on the margins of existence. The Christian sacrificed the possibility of material possessions because such a sacrifice helped the very poor to rise a bit above the margins separating them from starvation. There are still certain places in the modern world where starvation or near starvation persists, but it is not a typical situation in our own social-economic system. When we talk about poverty in the United States we must keep in mind that the word is being used very analogously, in comparison with, let us say, the poverty of Ireland in the mid-nineteenth century, when millions starved to death. It is not at all any criticism of the campaign of the black militants for a greater share of American wealth to say that the living conditions of most blacks today would have seemed to the Irish immigrants in New York, Boston, Philadelphia, and Chicago eight or nine decades ago as conditions of abundance if not wealth. Most of the black poor, for example, still have houses with heat and running water and many of the Irish immigrants did not. Voluntary poverty in the thirteenth century was hailed as virtue because it was thought, quite correctly, to make it possible for some people not to starve who otherwise would starve. But the technology of the modern world has made it possible for the first time in history for there to be an adequate supply of wealth. No one need starve, save through the incompetence of leadership.

Secondly, ancient theories of poverty assume a simple technique of redistribution; if the rich man gave up his wealth and sold his goods for the poor, then the poor would benefit. But the distribution in our complex world economy is such that your sacrifice or my sacrifice is not likely to have much impact on the lives of the poor at all. Whether you own a Cadillac or a Chevrolet or a Toyota does not help the black poor. Indeed, it doesn't even help them very much if you put the difference between the Toyota and the Cadillac into some form of charity for the poor. The problems in the United States are not a lack of adequate resources, but rather, the absence of a system for distribution of goods and training of personnel to fight the effects of poverty. Similarly, whether the American child eats his dessert or not has little relevance to the problems of India or Africa, even though he may be adjured to think of the starving millions. The complexities of the world distribution process are such that the United States cannot ship its vast surplus of grain to India as a gift, because such a gift would destroy their economy and cause even more poverty and starvation.

Obviously, the world's economic system needs major readjustment to eliminate such an absurdity, but the readjustment is a complex task which requires a great deal of economic sophistication. If one wished to dedicate one's life to the solution

of the problems of international economics, it would indeed be
a worthy vocation, but one's personal poverty is likely to have
absolutely no impact on these problems.

A third assumption on which the older theory of poverty
seems to rest is that most wealth has been amassed by immoral means, by the exploitation of the poor or the defenseless.
I certainly would not want to argue that the great fortunes
of our time or even many of the lesser fortunes have been
put together without substantial violation of other peoples' rights,
but it is also possible in the modern world to become financially
comfortable, wealthy, even very wealthy, not only without ex-
ploiting other human beings, but actually in the process of
rendering to them very useful and important services. You
can still make money by cheating the poor, but you can also
make money, and probably more of it, by making goods and
services available to the poor, and indeed by improving the
condition of the poor so that they are no longer poor and can
afford to buy your goods and services.

The final assumption of the old theory of poverty is the
notion that if one spends one's money on anything that one
absolutely doesn't need, one is going to cheat or injure those
who are less fortunate, but as a matter of fact, just the opposite
is true in contemporary society. If all of us just bought what
we absolutely need, the American economy would collapse and
the American unemployment rate would skyrocket. It can be
said without any exaggeration at all that we absolutely must
purchase luxuries if a massive increase in poverty is not to
take place. A situation like this would be inconceivable to the
older spiritual writers and seems to be almost incredible to
many modern commentators too.

I do not want to deny, however, the validity of the charisma
of voluntary poverty. It is, under some circumstances, unques-
tionably an effective form of witness bearing.* Such witness

---

* I'm not talking here about the vow of poverty, for whatever canonical
power or ascetical value it may have; it has nothing to do with material
deprivation, as those who are still poor in our nation and our world understand these things.

bearing, first of all, manifests the Christian's refusal to let material goods interfere with his pursuit of a vision which transcends, if it does not deny, material possessions. It also indicates the Christian sympathy with those who are poor, and a desire to serve Christ as he is to be found in the least of the brothers. Finally, as a form of personal service, it can be very meaningful in the lives both of those who serve and those who are served. But with all these things being said, it is still nevertheless true: the plight of the poor in this country is much more likely to be improved by the man who leads a campaign against current welfare practices than the one who sells his goods and goes and lives with the poor. The danger of posing and playing a game is very strong for those who wish to identify with the poor. They may be merely working out in practice their own alienations and turning the poor into objects to serve and justify these alienations. The British movie *Up the Junction* serves as a very pointed illustration of the harm a rich girl can do to poor people when she decides to pretend that she is one of them; a superficial pretense at poverty is in its own way every bit as bad as depriving the poor of their goods, because pretense deprives them of their privacy and dignity as persons.

Conceding that in some circumstances the spirit may move certain individuals to voluntary lives of extreme poverty, one must assert that this is not the normal way for most Christians and that we are still faced with the problem of what the underlying truth of the poverty tradition implies for the modern world.

I'm inclined to think that the underlying truth is very simple, but that it's applications are very complex. The truth is that the Christian witness in relationship to material goods is the appropriate use of them and even their appropriate enjoyment; and the complex question of application is: what does *appropriate* mean?

In an age of limited resources, appropriate use of goods meant the kind of material poverty that St. Francis of Assisi prescribed for some Christians, and a very cautious and frugal use of material goods for most Christians; but the emphasis of physical deprivation as appropriate was relevant only when the economic and social system was such that one could, by depriving oneself, serve others. Such self-deprivation has much less meaning today, if indeed it has any. One can serve the poor not so much by giving up material things, but rather, by devoting one's time and energy to social reform. So the virtue of poverty, translated into modern terms, demands minimally that the Christian be committed to those social reforms which are necessary to eliminate the institutional causes of poverty and suffering. However, as the rather unsuccessful War on Poverty demonstrated, it is not yet altogether clear what kinds of institutional reforms are going to be most successful.

Sacrifice of material goods for the sake of sacrifice is not appropriate for the Christian. It only becomes appropriate when it serves some higher end, and in a society organized like ours, higher ends are rarely served. A few of us may have the special charisma of total poverty. Most of the rest of us would be better advised to dedicate ourselves to social and economic reform and to more extensive production in goods and services rather than redistribution of what exists.

But if deprivation for it's own sake is not a good thing, we are still forced to face the problem of what is the appropriate use of material things. It may be possible to lay down some tentative norms:

1. Material goods exist to free the human spirit; thus anything that reduces drudgery or challenges the human spirit is appropriate for the Christian.

2. Material possessions are designed to decrease our worries, not increase them; thus any material goods which cause us a great deal of anxiety or confusion are not appropriate and one should either rid one's self of the goods or change one's attitude about them. No one is enthused about the first scratches on a new car but he who allows his peace and tranquillity to be disturbed for a long time by those first scratches is not

engaging in the appropriate use of his possessions. Furthermore, compulsive installment buying or compulsive living beyond one's means is inappropriate in the Christian life. Both these forms of behavior imprison the spirit rather than free it, and multiply our worries rather than decrease them.

3. Material possessions should be bought to be used and not merely as compensation for psychic frustrations. As I indicated in an earlier chapter, the compensatory function of material possessions is not necessarily a bad thing, but the housewife with a new dress, the photographer with a new lens, or the parish priest with a new television ought to be sure before he makes his purchase that it is something that he really intends to use.

4. Our possessions should not dominate us; that is to say, we have to avoid the piling up of goods which are not used but which become an immense burden to us. The Christian ought to be able to travel light. Traveling light is a state of mind, an ability to use goods in such a way that our concern over them does not dominate us. But also, traveling light is more than just a state of mind, as the agony that most of us go through when we have to move demonstrates. We all have more things than we can ever possibly use. The more we have, the more difficult it is for us to dominate our possessions instead of being dominated by them. Here is perhaps the most important truth the tradition of poverty can teach us. Material things may be excellent, they may be made for our enjoyment, but unless we impose limitations on our amassing of them, they will overwhelm us.

5. Our possessions are meant to be enjoyed, which is perhaps merely another way of saying that we should only possess those things which we are able to use. As an owner of an on-going series of motorboats, none of which ever worked very well, I have always been profoundly envious of the owners of the large white cabin cruisers which dominate marinas. But it has occurred to me frequently that most of these boats seem to stay in the marina. Even on the most perfect of summer

weekends, half the boats in any given harbor are tightly shut-
tered, their owner nowhere in sight. My ancient and moribund
Chris-Craft is in fact worth more than these splendid yachts,
because the Chris-Craft is used—when it works—and these yachts
are not. They may be status symbols or they may be means
of self-deception, but they never should have been bought
unless their owners intended to use them and to enjoy them.*

6. Finally, having made our own set of decisions about what
the appropriate use of material goods is for us, we have no
right to use our decisions as norms for setting judgment on
others. Given the complexities of the modern world and the
infinite variety of styles available to the Christian, only the
narrow-minded bigot wishes to impose his style on others. We
may well say that the Cadillac, or a vacation in Antigua, or
an elaborate stereo-tape system would not be appropriate for
us, but to condemn others because they judge that it is appropriate for them runs against the gospel injunction that we
should not judge lest we be judged. Exploitation we can condemn; the failure to use the goods that one possesses, we can
pity; becoming a slave to material goods, we can reject; but
we have no right to sit in judgment on anyone else. Those
opponents of clerical celibacy who say celibacy is meaningless
if it is not accompanied by the charisma of poverty seem to
misunderstand both charismas. Both give a certain kind of
freedom, though celibacy provides far greater freedom for the
servants of the People of God than does poverty. It is also
true that celibacy sometimes has served as an excuse for greed
and avarice, for the piling up of material possessions beyond
all appropriate limits. The two charismas are still not linked,
either by logic or by the demands of reality, and those who
wish to link them would be better advised not to try and budget
the Holy Spirit's time for him.

But is there anything to be learned from the great master
of poverty, Francis of Assisi, which is relevant for the modern

* Any owner of an unwanted cruiser who is desirous of giving it away
should contact the writer.

world? There certainly is, though we must look at the important thing about Francis. The important thing was not that he lacked material possessions but rather that he was a vigorously joyful and happy man. He was able to relate to the material world in such a way that he was free to be happy. He manifested the radical freedom from restraints and constraints that every Christian ought to enjoy. Poverty did not make Francis self-righteous, it did not make him anxious, it did not make him insecure, it simply made him free. He did not say that the things of this world were evil, but he did assert, as all Christians must, that there was a world beyond this world, a world of promise which would not destroy the present world but perfect it, that world of promise was where the heart of Francis and the heart of every true Christian must be. In the case of Francis himself, his radical freedom was best manifested by owning nothing himself. There are some who bear the same witness at any time in Christian history, though, as we have suggested before, such witness may have been more economically necessary in one time than in another. For the rest of us, our radical freedom is manifest in the responsible use of those things which we possess in stewardship. One is tempted to say that the witness of responsible stewardship is both more difficult and more necessary in an affluent society than it was in a society living on the margins of poverty. The use of material goods to enhance, rather than curtail, our radical freedom as sons of God is a complex task, both intellectually and practically. We cannot write off material goods as would the Manichee. But neither can we agree with the Pelagian that there is absolutely no danger in material possessions. We must steer a precarious middle course that affirms the necessity and the value of enjoying the goods of this world and at the same time warns of the danger of giving ourselves over as slaves to these material goods.

We have noticed in previous chapters how pervasive in man's spiritual life is the tendency to swing from one extreme to another. The puritan becomes a libertine, the purely rational man "tunes out," the foolishly brave man turns into a coward. So too, the Ebenezer Scrooges of this world, who are so fearful to spend money, become themselves, or generate in others, exactly the opposite extreme—wild, irresponsible spending. There are a number of reasons for this oscillation between extremes. The man who rejects and loathes himself does not trust his own ability to steer a middle course, because middle courses involve ambiguities and uncertainties and apparent contradictions. If he cannot have one extreme, then he will surely have the other.

But some of those who have been trusted with teaching the Christian tradition oftentimes have missed the point completely. Whereas the Christian should be teaching the glories and beauties of sexual love, he has often contented himself with warning of its dangers. Although the Christian should be insisting that physical pleasures are indispensable to life, he has often allowed himself to be tricked into warning of the dangers of material pleasures. While the Christian should be praising the goods that God has lavished on the world (as St. Francis surely did), he is frequently found warning people that they ought to live on as little material goods as possible.

The mistake is the refusal to believe that the good news is as good as it sounds. If we are really willing to take our Christian insights seriously, we would believe that the best way to campaign against sexual excess is to praise the dignity and beauty and pleasurability of human love. The best way to prevent people from throwing themselves into a mad libertine search for pleasure is not to warn them against pleasure, but to praise it as an anticipation of the resurrection. The best way to guide men to the proper use of material things is to praise their splendors as part of God's mighty and gracious universe. Surely we do not have to be very sophisticated psychologists to understand that men are much more likely to treat something with respect if you tell them that it is good than they are if you tell them it is evil. While the Lord gave us many examples of this as the best way to teach, we really aren't quite yet prepared to believe him, for the good news is still too good to be true.

My friend John Hotchkin of the Bishops' Committee on Ecumenical and Interreligious Affairs has insisted repeatedly that what is most needed today is a Christian materialism. He argues that we must repent of all our condemnations of materialism because these have clearly not been adequate to prevent the abuse of material things. Only, he insists, when we are able to praise material things enough, will men realize that they must treat them with reverence and respect. He adds, that it may even be necessary for the good Christian literally to wallow around in his material goods in order that he may assert their goodness.

A Porsche, is a splendid mechanism and one that ought to be greatly admired as a reflection in its own way of God's beauty and goodness. Not every Christian should have a Porsche (indeed, I suspect that a lot of those who have probably ought not to have one), but a Porsche is still a good thing and it is meant to be enjoyed. If it becomes an end unto itself, if it imprisons its owner, if it dominates his life, if it takes him away from his family and his friends and his career, then that beautiful piece of machinery would be better off in a junk heap. If, on the other hand, he feels guilty about it, is not able to enjoy it, he probably needs a psychiatrist. For the Christian, the Porsche is a splendid toy to be played with and enjoyed in anticipation of even greater playfulness and more splendid toys in the world yet to come.

9. *But We Can't Walk Alone*
(CHASTITY)

Wandering can be lonely; we need a road map, confidence in ourselves, hope that we will find our goal, courage, discretion, the ability to enjoy ourselves, and light baggage if we're not going to be lost in our wanderings. Because of all the complexities involved, we are strongly tempted to go it alone, to give up on the possibility of finding anyone with whom to share our wandering. If it is such a difficult and complicated task, traveling companions are simply going to make it worse. Yet we merely have to walk out on the highway to discover that we are not traveling alone. Quite the contrary, we are surrounded by fellow wanderers. God has played somewhat of a nasty trick on us, he has given us no choice; either our fellow wanderers become traveling companions who help us in our wanderings and whom we help or they become roadblocks to our traveling.

As much as we would like to do it, we cannot go it alone. The choice of the Fathers of the desert who wandered off into the boondocks and tried to live by themselves might appear attractive. It is still worth remembering, however, that even on the supposedly inaccessible pillar of Simeon Stylites, he couldn't escape from his fellow human beings who came out to ask him all kinds of pertinent and impertinent questions, the answers to which could then be recorded on paper and reread in refectories of religious houses for a thousand years or more. In whatever presumably quiet section of the hereafter to which St. Simeon has been assigned, he must be faintly amused and somewhat embarrassed (if embarrassment is permitted in the hereafter) at those tens of thousands of refectory readings.

So even though we may be lonely on our wanderings, it is quite impossible to be alone. Jean Paul Sartre's "other people" are all around us; they bring us into the world, they marry us, we bring them into the world, they work with us, provide our food and clothing, come to us with their problems or seeking our services. They're not going to go away and we might just as well learn to get along with them, although it must be confessed that until this point in human history in any case, man has not made a very good job of getting along with his fellow wanderers.

The Church was intended to be a community of wanderers, a band of travelers who had such great love and trust for one another that they could facilitate each other's wandering, make it more confident, more certain, and more enjoyable. The fellowship of journeyers that is the Church was supposed to be so attractive that everyone else in the world would perceive that its members would know the best way to get to the end of the journey and flock to join.

The Church is not yet that kind of fellowship; it does not provide all the encouragement its own members need and looks less than irresistibly attractive to those who have not yet joined it. There ought not to be any loneliness in the Church; at least there ought to be less than there is anywhere else. But the difference between the level of loneliness in the Church and outside of it is so minute that it is barely visible to the naked eye. We are still, it is to be feared, very much in the state of primitive Christianity.

Loneliness may well be the most terrifying emotion the human being can experience, at least over the long run. Other fears may be more horrendous for a brief period of time; loneliness persists and its long-run impact on the human personality is deadly. The lonely man feels that he is important to no one, that it would matter to no one if he died and that in fact he does not exist. The lonely man is aware—painfully, poignantly aware—that he is part of the walking dead; physical death would seem far more attractive than the permanent psychic death of loneliness.

Yet we are only lonely if we choose to be; we *join* the lonely crowd; we do not have to be alone, all the modern existentialist pessimists notwithstanding. If we refuse to seize the opportunities of our lives then we have deliberately chosen loneliness.

In one of the episodes of the superlative of television drama, "Star Trek," Captain Kirk and company are transported from other space to the O.K. Corral in 1894. To their astonishment, they become the Clanton gang the day of the famous shoot-out with the Erp brothers and Doc Holliday. Although they are conscious of the unreality of their situation, they begin to believe it. Their attempts to escape fail and they prepare almost eagerly for the gunfight. But in the nick of time the resourceful Mr. Spock saves the day. He points out to his colleagues that the whole thing is an illusion and, even worse, "illogical." "Star Trek's" staff can only be killed at the O.K. Corral if they are willing to believe in the reality of the illusion in which they have been caught. They steadfastly reject the illusion as unreal and illogical and the bullets of the imaginary Erp brothers and the equally imaginary Doc Holliday can do them no harm. Only if they lose their grasp on reality and permit themselves to become enmeshed in the illusion will they destroy themselves by believing in the reality of the imaginary bullets that are being fired at them. So Kirk, Spock, Scott, McCoy, and Chekov face down the brothers Erp in the O.K. Corral and remain completely unharmed as the latter blaze away with their six-shooters; needless to say, Spock was right.

Someone could write a book with "Star Trek" as a modern

morality play where Captain Kirk is the Christ figure and Mr. Spock is a priest figure. In fact, maybe someday I will write such a book, since the "Star Trek" philosophy is a profoundly affirmative and hopeful one, rooted as it is in reality, goodness, generosity, and love; but in this volume I merely want to cite the wisdon of Mr. Spock at the O.K. Corral. If we believe in illusions long enough, they become real. If we have the courage to defy the illusions, then the .45-caliber bullets coming from the guns of illusion can do us no harm. If we choose to define ourselves as alone, to hide behind fear and timidity, and accept loneliness, then loneliness, which is at root an illusion, becomes a reality far more deadly than the guns of Wyatt and Morgan Erp and Doc Holliday.

It might be wondered what loneliness and Mr. Spock have to do with the virtue of chastity. Chastity is that virtue which, in the Christian tradition, guides us in the wise use of the sexual dimension of our personality. It is not, despite some puritan fanatics to the contrary, a virtue which turns Christians into a third sex who know not desire or passion. It does not make us angels who are unaware of our own bodies or the bodies of others. It ought not even to make us think that the spontaneous sexual urges which are so much a part of our life are either dirty or irresistible temptations. Chastity, rather, is that virtue which enables us to channel our sexual energies in such a way that they enrich and reinforce an open, trusting, and loving human life.

There has been a lot about sex in this volume, because there's a lot of sex in human life, some of it healthy and much of it unhealthy. The unhealthiness of sex can be traced to our fears and our misunderstandings. We do not see it as a sublimely good and powerful human energy. We cannot and ought not try to control this energy completely but, nonetheless, it must be shaped and integrated into the broader context of our personality and its life project.

Sex, then, is an antidote to loneliness, because it creates in man a powerful drive to break out of the barriers of isolation and fear which he has built around himself. Sex simply cannot be enjoyed alone; even autoeroticism is directed at others, though the others may exist only in our fantasies. Sex is relational, it fiercely resists loneliness; and, given half a chance, will overcome it.

The various psychoanalytic traditions which have sprung from the work of Sigmund Freud argue about whether the "pleasure principle" of the "libido" is distinct from man's sexual energies. The argument is not an unimportant one theoretically, but it is surely beyond the scope of the present volume. It suffices to say here that all human pleasure is not sexual, at least in the sense that the word is normally used; thus, for example, a good steak dinner is not ordinarily a sexual experience. Nevertheless, most pleasures which are not in themselves sexual are so closely related to the sexual dimension of the human personality that they can readily become very sexual in tone. The steak dinner with someone with whom we are deeply in love can become a powerful sexual experience (one remembers, for example, the famous eating scene in the movie version of *Tom Jones*). Furthermore, there are certain other kinds of physical pleasures, particularly those where there is great sensible beauty involved—music, art, beautiful scenery are examples that come to mind—that seem intimately connected with the sexual dimensions of the personality, so that it is very difficult to separate enjoying them from a sexual reaction. Finally, since we are inevitably and totally physical (that is not to say, of course, that we are not totally spiritual), every relationship with those who have bodies necessarily involves our body and therefore is sexual. Only if we were both archangels could it possibly be any different.

The Manichee mentality is shocked at the thought that sex is everywhere. But the Manichee and the Calvinist can take this problem up, if not with Sigmund Freud, then with the God who made man male and female and built sex into their personalities from the very beginning and from the tiniest chromosomes of their being.

The idea that physical attractiveness shared by two people (and there is no human being who is not physically attractive) necessarily leads to the marriage bed or homosexual behavior has been a self-fulfilling prophecy for centuries. If the sexual dimension of the personality is felt to be too big for man to control, then when that dimension involves us in powerful urges, we quickly abandon hope of focusing these urges in accordance with the norms of the reality in which we find ourselves. If men and women believe that sex will destroy them, then, of a certainty, sex will destroy them. Gonadic determinism can easily be refuted both by theory and by empirical data, but it is firmly rooted in the human consciousness and has been so for centuries. Under such circumstances, human beings, particularly those who take the advice of certain spiritual writers and spiritual directors seriously, feel that they must either rigorously repress their sexual instincts almost to the extent of pretending that they are sexless, or give themselves over to a life of what used to be called "unbridled lust." The fact that the definitions and the theories permit no middle ground guarantees that in practice there will be no middle ground.

Furthermore, since man's sexual dimension is so insistent and so pervasive, sex feelings become marvelous justification for our own assumed worthlessness. Only a worthless person could be plagued by dirty fantasies and ideas. And if, on occasion, one should engage in sexual behavior that violates the realities in which one finds oneself, then abject worthlessness is certain beyond a doubt. It is then easy for the opposite reaction to set in. If one is indeed worthless, then one may as well give oneself over to worthless activities and enjoy them as much as one can. One is not good enough to be sexless and, therefore, the only other alternative is to be a Don Juan or a nymph.

An alternative model, and one in keeping with both the Christian tradition and the contemporary behavioral science notion of man, would be to argue that man's sexuality is merely the force inside the human person urging him to break out of the physical and psychic loneliness into which he is slipping.

Those "dirty thoughts" and "unruly passions" are merely a way
the Almighty has devised of saying to man, "It is not good
for you to be alone." They do not necessarily say, "You must
find yourself a wife," or, "You must have intercourse before the
day is over," or, "Homosexuality can be fun." But they do say,
"You are a composite of mind and body, of spirit and flesh,
don't you ever forget it, and don't you ever try to cut yourself
off from others who are both spirit and flesh."

Because sexuality is such an overwhelmingly powerful force,
and because we have so little understanding of or confidence
in ourselves, the signals it sends us are likely to be confused
and erratic. The realities of who we are and who the other
is may be at variance with the obvious and explicit contents
of the message of our sexual urges. Thus a man who is strongly
attracted to a woman other than his wife may be receiving
explicit messages which say, "Seduce her," or, "Rape her." But
if he is mature enough and confident enough of himself and
honest and trusting enough in his relationship with his wife, he
will be able to discover that there are implicit messages in
his sexual urges which are not at variance with the reality
of his relationships. These messages may be saying, "She is
indeed an attractive woman, but because of who you are and
who she is, no meaningful relationship is possible," or, "You
are very lonely and the reason you feel such awful urges
toward this woman is that your relationship with your wife
is so unsatisfactory; in part, at least, because you are afraid to be
open and honest with her," or, "You have so repressed all the
humanity that is in you by your simple-minded and compulsive
devotion to your career that these strange and frightening urges
come upon you because you have kept welled up inside almost
all human emotion," or, "Reality is such that you and this woman
can have a deeply meaningful friendship that may be profoundly sexual, but which will not drive you to genital activity
and which will enhance all your relationships with other people
rather than weakening them."

These messages, combinations of them, and many other messages are being fed into our personality constantly by the sexual dimension of that personality. The underlying message of all the signals is, "You cannot be alone, you cannot hide; try as you might, that self-loathing which impedes your giving of yourself to others and accepting them back is destroying the human being in you."

No generalized statements can be made about the human sexual reactions that are valid in all circumstances. You cannot run to the textbooks or to confessors for "answers" in any area of human behavior, but particularly in one as volatile as this. This is not suggesting, Heaven protect us, that there are no absolute standards regulating sexual relationships; adultery, fornication, exploitation are wrong and are also dys-functional to psychic health. But there is an almost infinite number of possible human relationships and possible human emotions for which the clear moral principles provide no immediately obvious guide. The simple-minded spiritual writers who say, avoid all dangers—by which they mean, repress all emotions—are no help at all, because they refuse to recognize the ambiguity and the obscurity of the human condition.

Such simple-minded "authorities" will insist that unless their rule of avoiding anything that might possibly be dangerous is followed, we may certainly make mistakes. Hopefully, mistakes have been sufficiently discussed in the previous chapter, but it is still necessary here to say that if such advice were followed in matters sexual, the human race would have stopped existing long ago.

The important issue at stake in this discussion is whether we have enough confidence in ourselves to focus our sexual energies within the limitations of "reality." By reality, I mean the web of valid relationships and commitments which constitutes the social and psychological environment in which we live. Does the priest believe that he is capable of keeping his commitments to the Church and to celibacy and still have

strong and passionate friendships with other human beings of
both sexes? Is he confident enough of his own goodness, the
maturity of his judgments, and his knowledge of his own personality strengths and weaknesses that he can enjoy these relationships, grow in them, be opened and trusting to his partners
in the relationships and at the same time become a better, instead
of a poorer, priest? Does he realize that such strong human
relationships will necessarily involve deep sexual feelings which
will not at all condemn him to either homosexuality or intercourse with the people for whom he has these feelings? Is he
willing to admit to himself that some woman can have immense
power over him without his having to jump into bed with her?
Can he say to himself that there are some women who turn him
into butter as soon as they walk into the room? Can he thoroughly enjoy this power they have over him and become a better
man and a better priest because of it? If he cannot give positive
answers to all of these questions, then I very much fear that
the priest is quite inadequate as a priest and a poor risk for
celibacy, particularly at the present time.

I deliberately have chosen the example of the priest, who
does not engage in genital activity, to illustrate the point I'm
trying to make; we either permit ourself to enjoy our sexuality
within the limitations of the reality in which we find ourselves
and then enjoy it as much as is prudent (as we defined prudent
in Chapter 7) or we attempt to repress our sexuality and mess
ourselves up badly. Sex is meant for enjoyment and if we do
not enjoy it, then it can very well destroy us. Prudent enjoyment
is the *only* way to prevent it from destroying us.

Sex is an extraordinarily powerful dimension of the human
personality which forces us to face reality and forces us to trust
others. Sexuality can only be rewarding when it's enjoyed in
a relationship of trust and openness. The more open and honest
we can be with the one to whom we are attracted, the more
pleasurable the sexual experience is and the more secure are
the contexts of reality in which it is being enjoyed. Yet most

people's sexual relationships are frustrating and most marriages, even very good marriages, are far less satisfying than they might easily be. It has always seemed somewhat surprising to this particular celibate how little meaningful communication there is about sex between most husbands and wives. There may be a great deal of talk (though even relatively few marriages, it seems to me, have much talk about sex) but there isn't much in the way of communication. Since the potential rewards in terms of sheer physical pleasure are so great in a harmonious sexual adjustment, one is forced to conclude that the fears which prevent spouses from discussing their sexual activity must be extraordinarily powerful. The insecurities, the timidities, the uncertainties about one's own sexuality are so great that we willingly give up the possibilities of great joy rather than take the risks of the self-disclosure that is necessary for such joy.

The low level of sexual satisfaction in many, if not most, marriages gives us some idea of the rather primitive state of the human race in its evolution toward trust and friendship. If passion can die so quickly because of fear, then we must concede that fear is still far more powerful in the world than trust. Every cell of the human body demands that a man be open and trusting toward his wife and she toward him. The most powerful physical pleasure that we can experience drives us toward trust, yet fear very easily and rather quickly overcomes it.

Most marriages are not "bad" marriages, they are not aimed at the divorce courts, and they aren't even between people that are basically incompatible. The greatest tragedy of marriage is not that some break up, or not even that others become stony and cold. The most tragic marriages are those that have everything going for them. They could so easily become tremendously enriching, both physically and emotionally, to both partners. But they don't quite make it as well as they easily might because the partners are afraid. Husband and wife reach a level of sexual adjustment that keeps passion under control, but they are afraid to let passion become the motive for more openness and mutual growth and to let mutual growth in its turn make passion far more rewarding. As a result, the two of them "go their own ways," the wife to her children and her homemaking duties, and the husband to his career. The level of sexual reward and of personal growth levels off and then slowly declines, though the husband and wife would claim that theirs is still a very "happy" marriage. Up to a point, it is, but the tragedy is that it could be so much happier.

I suspect that most of the casual sex which happens in upper-middle-class professional society results from the fact that the spark has gone out of the relationship between husband and wife. The physical and emotional kicks of having temporarily a new partner reassures a person that he or she still is capable of sexual enjoyment; but in the casual relationship, there is no need for the enjoyment to be anything more than transitory, no need to build up an enduring relationship, no need for openness and trust, no need for honesty or self-disclosure, no need for the painful effort required to build friendship and love. Neither is there any hope that there can be friendship and love. Casual sex, because of its very novelty and secretiveness is more fun than that provided by a marriage which is not really bad but not really very good either. However, married sex which flows from and reinforces an authentic and developing friendship makes the transitory thrills of casual adultery seem mild in comparison. The only trouble is, the casual adulterer has no basis for comparison.

I must say that I have been intrigued by the "sex in the afternoon" phenomenon. It is no secret that a fair number of business and professional men manage to find time periodically during the afternoon of their working day to engage in some casual extramarital relaxation. It is also no secret that perhaps a smaller number of their wives manages to do the same thing back in their suburban homes (my hunch is that wives are less likely to do it than their husbands not because they are any less lonely and frustrated, but simply because opportunities are more available for the businessman downtown than for the wife in the suburbs). I have found myself wondering, if "sex in the afternoon" is so enjoyable—and I have certainly no reason to think that it would not be—why more business or professional men and their wives do not arrange to have secret afternoon rendezvous. The response to such a question—and those whom I have with innocent demeanor asked it are usually quite surprised—is that, well, there simply isn't any time for it, they are too busy with their jobs and their wives are too busy with their obligations back in the suburbs. What I interpret this to mean is that both husband and wife are too busy to work on an enduring relationship, though not too busy to enjoy a casual one. If this be true, the real problem isn't business or time; the difficulty is that an enduring relationship requires effort, patience, attention, self-disclosure, and trust. Of these, both husband and wife are still afraid. If they were truly chaste, they would break out of the prisons of fear and uncertainty and insecurity and inadequacy which they have built for themselves and set to work at the difficult task of creating mutual trust. The real unchastity is not in casual adultery, it is in fearful refusal to labor for a mutuality of trust.

There are all kinds of masks, most of them made of strong armor, behind which we can hide our sexual loneliness and fear. We can be the great lover or the strong, silent type, or the cave man, or the flirt, or the bitch, or the frigid wife, or the apathetic husband, or the experience-seeking cleric. We can be the sophisticate or the vulgar locker-room humorist, we can be clinically frank or puritanically prim. Behind these masks there lurks a single emotion—fear—fear of our maleness, fear of our femaleness, fear of our humanity, fear to disclose ourselves, fear of failure, fear of rejection, fear of ridicule, fear of losing control, fear of being cheated, fear of "not knowing what it's all about," and fear of missing something. Curiously enough, we don't seem to be afraid of loneliness, at least not to the extent that it is necessary to face our sexuality realistically, to admit that it is a power we can never fully control or fully understand. We are afraid to try to enjoy it as much as we can in the circumstances in which we find ourselves. The Lord must shake his head in dismay; he has put this awesome pleasure at our disposal in order to help us overcome our loneliness and we resolutely refuse to use it for the purpose for which it was intended.

I have argued in another book that sex and friendship are inseparable. Sex can never be very rewarding in the human species unless it occurs in the context of friendship, and friendship came into the human experience through the marriage relationship. Only if they were friends could man and his mate bear to endure each other. Friendship had its origins in the mating relationship and all friendship is rooted in our bodies and hence is pervasively sexual. Nonetheless, friendship can transcend sex and need not be genital. The distinction is so obvious that one might almost think it hardly worth mentioning, if it were not for the fact that most people do not believe it and do not live according to it. Like most everything else in the paradise in which the Lord God has set us, sex is too good to be true.

There is too much loneliness in the world and correspondingly there is not enough good sex. We who are Christians ought to dedicate our lives both to the elimination of loneliness and the improvement of sex. The Church is created in the image of the sexual union. The better that union is, the better the Church will appear; and correspondingly, the stronger and deeper and richer the friendships are within the Church, the more attractive the Church will be to others. Given the reciprocal relationship between the Church and friendships, our convictions about the nature of friendship should make the Church stronger and the Church in its turn should make our friendships stronger. This benign circle has not really been set in motion yet, at least not in rapid motion. One supposes that this is proof that we haven't gotten very far into Christianity yet. As we progress, as we love each other more and radiate that love into the world about us, then the awesome, terrible evil of loneliness will diminish. Diminish it ought, for, as Mr. Spock in "Star Trek" would put it, it is an illusion and therefore "it is not logical."

10. *Terran, Take Me to Your Discussion Leader*
(OBEDIENCE)

Since our wandering is necessarily in a community, there must be in the community some co-ordination of efforts. The co-ordination has to be kept at a minimum to allow the most possible freedom and creativity in the development of our life projects, but the minimum is measured by what is required for the common good of our fellowship. Co-ordination is required in order that our co-operative wandering effort might be facilitated. Without co-ordination of some sort, co-operation is simply not possible. Unfortunately, at most times in human history co-operation has been at sword point or gunpoint, or anathema point. It was assumed that man was bad, or at least stupid. The only way you could get him to co-operate with his fellowmen was by either physical or moral force.

Occasionally, men like Jean Jacques Rousseau suggested that you really didn't need any co-ordination and if you left man to himself, permitting each man to seek his own best interests, some marvelous harmony of co-operation would emerge. In recent years (let's say the last two centuries) the idea has emerged that you obtain co-operation only by obtaining consent. The power of authority depends ultimately on the consent of those among whom the authority is exercised. In the complex, dynamic industrial society in which we live, this principle, whatever its metaphysical and moral excellence may be, has also become a hard-nosed maxim of practical efficiency. If you can't get the maximum co-operation from those with whom you are working, then you are going to have a very inefficient and ineffective work group. Because of the need for accurate information and for complex skills, only a self-directing and professionally motivated team is able to man the critical positions in society. Hence the sacred arbitrary power of the past is forever dead and the ability to obtain operational consent is demanded of anyone who presumes to exercise leadership functions.

Within that fellowship of travelers called the Catholic Church, there is considerable talk about the crisis of authority, with certain elements trying desperately to preserve the absolutist authority of the past on the grounds that it is of divine origin (though it was a type of authority that the Lord himself never seems to have exercised). Others, on the contrary, wish to see all authority abolished and our fellowship of travelers governed "not by law but by love." Like many of the other theoretical arguments in the Church, this one is quite irrelevant. For, whatever the theoretical nature of the authority may be, it still must (in a complex modern institution) be exercised in a consensual fashion. Obedience in the modern world is *not* the virtue which inclines us to respond blindly and unthinkingly to whatever our leader says; it is, rather, that virtue which inclines us to enter into a responsible, co-operative relationship with those who are our colleagues. Blind assent to the leader may have been functional for a group when the problems were simple and society was uncomplicated, but it would be sinful, given the complexities and the chaos which the Church faces today, to respond with blind obedience. The Church needs intelligent and responsible co-operation. He who is not ready to give intelligent, responsible co-operation is actually disobedient, because he is frustrating the common purpose for which the members of the fellowship have come together.

The illusion seems to be abroad in the land that this new obedience is easier both for him who has authority and for those with whom he exercises authority. If the leader no longer has to make the decisions, but, rather, asks the questions and presides over the concensus, it is argued, there is really nothing much left for him to do. If his followers, instead of responding by doing exactly what they are told, are expected responsibly and intelligently to contribute their own ideas, their own information, or their own talent in shaping the common policy, there is not much sacrifice demanded of them; not nearly as much as that sacrifice of the intellect which, it is argued, blind obedience really demands.*

Anyone who has presided over or participated in a consensual and collegial group knows that far more is demanded both of the leader and the followers in such an arrangement. It is a relatively simple thing to give answers and then ruthlessly and rigorously demand that these answers be carried out. It is much more difficult to determine what the right questions are, then to ask these questions in an insistent way, and to demand that all of your colleagues focus the maximum amount of their energies on finding a common solution to the questions. It is also far more difficult to endure the agonies of dialogue and opinion exchange without giving up in despair and letting the loudest or the most aggressive carry the day. Government by group discussion is not easy for anybody, but in the modern world it is the only feasible kind of government. If one compares the Kennedy Administration, which was in great part a consensual and collegial one, with the Johnson Administration, which was far more arbitrary and authoritarian, one sees that the latter form leads to self-destructive blunders, while the former is more effective, if far more difficult. Those in the

---

* One priest once said to me, "Isn't it true, Father, that it's more virtuous to do something out of obedience than to do it because it seems to be the intelligent thing?" This seems to me to be a way of saying, isn't it more virtuous to be unintelligent than to be intelligent? I am constrained to reply, "No, it is not, not at least, that is, if you are a human being the Lord has given intelligence to."

Church who still wish to govern arbitrarily might do well to ponder the tragedy of the Administration of Lyndon Johnson: the biggest landslide victory in decades, the greatest social reforms of the twentieth century, and yet an Administration which ended in defeat and disgrace because there was no trust among the members of the President's staff, no trust of the people, and eventually no trust from the people.

Obedience, then, is that virtue which inclines us to co-ordinate with others the complex talents, knowledge, and skills which are necessary for a successful collegial administration. Obedience must be open, non-competitive, and intense. By open, I mean that we must not hold back our ideas for fear we will be criticized or suffer personal rejection because of them. One of the problems of collegiality in the Kennedy Administration was that popular reports attributed to some of the President's staff ideas which they advanced for the sake of discussion, but to which they were not necessarily committed. The press, after the missle crisis, reported that Ambassador Stevenson supported a very weak position, while Mr. Acheson supported a very "hawkish" stand. Such news leaks made it difficult for the Kennedy staff to feel perfectly free to investigate all possibilities, although later more detailed studies of the Cuban Crisis made it quite clear that there was a constant shifting of stands and positions as the various members of the team fed their own ideas and insights into the group dialogue. In a collegial group no one should have any fear that he will be criticized or ridiculed or rejected for any suggestion he may make.

If we must feel open enough to speak our mind even when we're anything but committed to the idea we express, so we also must be open enough to listen to what others are saying and to listen to the substance of what they say and not the categories in which they may express themselves. We must not turn down or reject or ridicule anyone because he seems to be saying something that is in disagreement with us or may sound absurd. We must, rather, patiently try to see the point that he is driving at and carefully consider it as a possible alternative to our own suggestions. Collegial dialogue requires as an absolute essential that we make a maximum effort to see things from the viewpoints of our colleagues.

Second, collegial activity must be non-competitive. Our goal must be to arrive at the best possible decision for the whole group and not to see our ideas triumph over someone else's or to see the leader approve us and reject him. This may be the toughest part of collegial government. The strongest demand of the virtue of obedience is that we be non-competitive in collegial activity. There is so much competition in our society and so much of it is rooted in the sibling relationships of our childhood that it is very difficult not to be competitive with those with whom we closely associate. We do not find it easy to rejoice when our colleagues catch us in a mistake, because their alertness protects all of us from making a mistake, and yet this is precisely what obedience requires of us.

There must be a great deal of security in the community for us to be able to afford to be non-competitive. My friend Peter Rossi used to say that in an academic collegium security was feasible as long as there was enough money to go around, but once the project grants came in short supply and there was competition for a lucrative project, then collegiality went down the drain. To some extent he is correct, yet I have also seen instances in academia where a collegial group threatened with a financial shortage rallied to help one another rather than panicking and becoming competitive because of the apparent shortage of funds. There was a great deal of enlightened self-interest in such a co-operation, because the collegium knew that it would either survive together or fall apart individually. The collegium had to be preserved.

We must also understand from the virtue of obedience that the brilliance of one member of the collegium reflects on the whole collegium. If a wife, for example, is smarter than her husband, the husband ought not to feel inferior, but rather should be proud and happy that he has a wife who is able to make a valuable contribution to the family fellowship. It is difficult for a husband to rejoice in the intelligence of a wife who is brighter than he, and yet this is precisely what obedience would demand of him in the contemporary world.

Finally, our obedience must be intense. We must commit ourselves enthusiastically to solving the problems of the group of which we are a part. The level of intensity depends both on the goals of the group and the seriousness of the problem, but our total person, with all its talents, must be involved in seeking the solution in whatever kind of commitment is appropriate in the particular circumstances. We cannot hold back or calculate as to how much we're going to get out of the particular relationship; if we have committed ourself to the relationship, then we must be prepared to give the best that we have under the circumstances to the relationship. The obedient man, then, is the one who is available to bring the best that he has to all the relationships in which he finds himself. He is one who is ready to respond to others when the reality of his relationship to others demands that he respond. Obedience in the family means that the husband is both physically and psychologically available to his wife when she needs him and wants him, and that she is similarly available to him. It also means that they are both available to their children when the children can legitimately demand a response and a commitment from them.

Obedience in our relationships with our friends means that we have no need to hold back from them or to fear them or to withhold our friendship from them or to punish them when they seem less than enthusiastic about us or, God forbid, to hinder them so that they will not excel us.

Obedience on our jobs means that we neither hide our own talents nor permit ourselves to be threatened by others' talents; we have no need to downgrade our colleagues or our superiors or our subordinates, nor any need to blame them for our own failures. We have committed ourselves to them in the common effort and we will give that common effort the best we reasonably can.

Obedience to the Church means that we do not use our colleagues (be they what Canon Law calls our inferiors or our superiors) as scapegoats for our own emotional frustration. We do not seek confrontations with them or attempt to escalate the level of these confrontations when they do occur as a solace for our own emotional needs. On the contrary, obedience in the Church means that we are available to our colleagues, seeking always grounds for dialogue and agreement, and that we are responsive to their availability to us. The obedient man, therefore, is not looking for the chance to battle, but rather, for an occasion to understand and to co-operate in the common effort.

Responsiveness is not the same thing as "doormat-ism." The former gives endlessly while the latter gives up. The former says what it thinks while the latter is quiet. The former believes that it is obliged to disagree when it feels disagreement and the other timidly avoids disagreement because it is unpleasant. The former respects leaders and colleagues so much that it is willing to respond to them intelligently and critically, while the latter condemns the colleagues so much that it does not even give them the benefit of any honest answer.

The obedient person, therefore, respects himself and gives his best to others while insisting that they are expected to give their best in return. The obedient man does not need to have his way, but rather, wants the community to make the best possible decision and will do all in his power to assure the maximum contribution of everyone else in the community.

This sort of obedience makes the blind obedience of the intellect, so extolled in our seminary days, look absurdly simple. "Obedience of the intellect" was basically irresponsible and the obedience described in this chapter is painfully responsible. Irresponsibility is always easier than responsibility. If anything, the irresponsibility of one who holds silence and does not contribute his best in the way of ideas and information and insight is worse than the irresponsibility of the one who refuses to have anything to do with a community. The latter does not pretend, while he who disagrees in silence pretends to go along. Half-hearted co-operation, in the modern world, is much worse than no co-operation at all.

It must be strongly insisted that the kind of obedience I am extolling in this chapter is not optional, it's not something that is nice because it sounds American and democratic, or is praiseworthy because it acknowledges the freedom and responsibility of individual members of a community. It is essential, because without it, a group is not likely to survive for long at a high level of productivity. There are few serious problems that the Catholic Church faces today that are not caused by the irresponsibility of passive, docile, silent, half-hearted co-operation. The culture and the structure of the Church still seem to favor such outmoded and dys-functional notions of obedience; and the refusal of the leaders and the followers in the Church to recognize that this sort of obedience is deadly dangerous has badly hampered the Church on its pilgrimage.

The team of astronauts, the pro football champions, the missile launching experts, the computer programmers, the combat squad are all collegial, because if they are not, they are going to fail and they know it. The risks are too great, the costs too high, the potential payoff too important for there to be any room for prima donnas in these activities—neither the prima donna who wants to give all the orders nor the prima donna who wants to do passively what others tell him to do. Similarly, on that wandering pilgrimage of ours—since we cannot go it alone—we must go with others in the most intelligent and co-operative fashion possible. There is too much at stake, too much can be lost, too many challenging demands are made upon us, there are too many difficult obstacles to overcome for us not to demand the best that is possible from all of our colleagues or for us to refuse to respond with our best when they demand it of us. Either we are obedient men, all of us together, or, as Benjamin Franklin put it, "We will all hang separately."

A whole new set of skills is required for this sort of obedience. Just as there is no room in the modern consensual collegium for the passive, dependent, quiet, docile amoeba of the past, so there is no room for his first cousin, the arrogant, aggressive, entrepreneur. There is an artistry to collegial activity; it requires its own protocol, its own rhetoric, its own sensitivity, and its own deep respect for the skills and insights of others. It absolutely demands that we present our ideas to the one who is most likely to disagree with them and to criticize them, since his insights are more important than anyone else's. He is the one most likely to prevent us from blundering and most likely to provide the reality check that is indispensable if our decisions are not to be ill-advised and precipitous. Instead of trying to convince the other members of our collegium that we are right, we must plead with them to do everything in their power to persuade us that we are wrong. This is not a pleasant or easy experience at best. As I have watched my colleagues of the National Opinion Research Center gleefully tear apart questionnaires over which I have labored painfully for weeks and months, I have often felt that it was much better back in the days of arbitrary and unilateral decision making. Yet, when it comes time to analyze the data collected by these questionnaires, I don't have much doubt. If it wasn't for the skills and insights—and the courage—of my colleagues in demolishing my questionnaires, the surveys would not be nearly as good as they are. (A whole lot of us then might be out of business—or as some would say, forced to seek an honest living.)

There is a certain similarity between a collegial group and a marriage relationship, or, to put the matter somewhat differently, marriage is simply the most intimate and demanding form of collegiality, the most difficult situation in which obedience is required. But the collegial work group, be it in university or church, is nonetheless a very intimate fellowship that requires openness, trust, confidence, courage, patience, sensitivity, and humor. It requires a delicate respect for both the skills and the weaknesses of those with whom we associate and an absolutely unshakable conviction that all of us together can do a far better job than each of us can do as an individual. It takes a strong person and a self-confident and self-respecting person to admit that he cannot do everything and that he can work much better if others are helping him.

While I can read a statistical table as easily as anyone else, I fear that never in this lifetime shall I be much good at the complexity of the more recent sociological methods, such as multiple regression analysis. If they take away from me my colleagues who are good at this kind of thing, I am a poorer sociologist. On the other hand, I can organize and write a report in about one fifth the time that any of the rest of them can. I may miss things occasionally, but my interpretations are always adequate and sometimes imaginative and ingenious. If they lose me, they lose one of the most able report writers in the land, to say nothing of a charming and occasionally successful fund raiser. I'm not at all ashamed to admit that I need them and they are not at all ashamed to admit that they need me. None of us is ashamed to admit that we, all of us, need such absolutely indispensable personnel as, for example, the administrative assistant to the director of the center.*

I do not want to argue that our battered and shifting team of social researchers is made up of completely obedient men. We have faults and failings and there are occasional dissatisfactions and conflicts one with another, but whatever our other faults may be, we are not stupid. Wanderers that we are, living by our wits in a highly marginal, though very exciting, operation, we know only too well that we absolutely need each other to survive. We are obedient out of pure necessity.

I suspect some readers will think that in this chapter I have been guilty to an even greater extent than I have in any of the others of perverting the meaning of a traditional concept. But we must ask ourselves what purposes these traditional concepts served. What I have suggested simply is that a reinterpretation of the meaning of a virtue requires that we first ask what

* Without able administrative assistants, all research centers collapse virtually at once.

the goal of this virtue originally was, and secondly, how the goal can best be served in the contemporary world.

The purpose of obedience is the co-ordination of human activity. It has no good in itself and takes its merit merely from the fact that it serves a definite end. If the goal of obedience is co-ordination of activities, then in modern society, obedience does not mean the giving or the obeying of orders; it means intelligent, responsible, available co-operation; it means a leader who demands the most responsible and intelligent kind of participation possible, even if this occasionally requires his colleagues to tell him that he's a darn fool; and it also means colleagues who are brave enough and vigorous enough and constant enough to collaborate as fully as they possibly can, even, and perhaps especially, when it means telling the discussion leader that he's a darn fool.

11. *So That's Where You Have Been Hiding* (PRAYER)

The assumption on which our wandering is based is that somewhere out there there is Someone. He's not only out there, but he's here with us too. Our wandering process is an exploration and a discovery; we find him out there to precisely the same extent that we find that he's already with us. The instant of discovery is much like that experienced by the apostles and disciples on the road to Emmaus. We know the Lord out there when we encounter him traveling with us in the breaking of the bread.

But the question is, of what sort is the One out there who is also in here? Is he a Thou? Can we talk to him? Does he talk to us? Is there any point in trying to get a conversation going? Some of our more sophisticated philosophers and theologians, having grown wise on the readings of logical positivism, are prepared to advance all kinds of reasons why it's possible neither to talk about the One out there, nor much less talk to him. They assure us that God talk is nonsense talk; up to a point, they may be correct, because we know so very little about that Ultimate toward which we are wandering and which is simultaneously wandering with us. Yet there are more things in heaven and earth than Horatio's philosophy dreamed of and infinitely more than the logic choppers could possibly dream of—if indeed they permit the possibility of dreams.

As Peter Berger has cleverly put it in his book *Rumors of Angels* (Doubleday, Garden City, N.Y., 1969), the same weapons the philosophers of language use on God talk can be used against them. If they wish to relativize all other discourse, then, to use one of Berger's chapter titles, it is fair to relativize the relativizers. While it may be true that those who are trained in the most skillful use of language are incapable of speaking about or to God, this does not at all indicate an answer to the question of whether there is a God or not, or whether he can be talked to or not. It merely indicates that logical positivists cannot talk to him or about him. In the next chapter, we will turn to some of the Rumors of Angels that Berger cites as evidence of, in his words, the fact that once the relativizers are relativized there is indeed Someone out there. In this chapter it is enough to assert that faith tells us that Graciousness is not to be denied and that we must dialogue with it. It is easy enough for us to talk, hoping that there is Someone out there who is listening, but he rarely seems to be speaking in return.

But the Lord as the Principle of Graciousness is speaking to us all the time through the physical world around us, through the instincts and the insights of the self and through the theophanies by which Graciousness manifests itself in a special way—and particularly in the central theophany in Christ Jesus. We must be able to listen to these revelations whether we hear them in the words of others, or in the signs of the times, or in the recesses of the self, or in the traditions of Jesus of Nazareth as carried down through time and space by the fellowship of wanderers that he founded. We must be able to listen to Graciousness speaking to us and to respond. Prayer is nothing more than listening to and responding to Graciousness as it speaks to us. Prayer is dialogue with Graciousness.

Our prayer affirms the unity between us and Graciousness and his manifestations, both in the content and in the manner of praying. What we say affirms unity and the fact that we say it reinforces what we have affirmed. Our prayer can be a quiet reflective meditation in which we listen to the voice of Graciousness in our own being and ponder over the implications of it as manifested in our experience, or it can be the prayer of public liturgy, in which we gather together with our fellow wanderers to mark the milestones on our journey in a public and solemn way.

In one act we affirm the Graciousness of each other, of the landscape through which we are traveling and of the One out there who is also in here that we are traveling both toward and with. Finally, dialogue with Graciousness takes place in what we used to call "private prayer," intimate conversation like a lover has with his beloved. For it is the conceit of human beings that the Principle of Graciousness out there and in here is in fact a lover who cares for us as tenderly as did the Prophet Hosea for his faithless wife. Since the love between a husband and a wife is the most rewarding and exciting relationship of which we are aware, we naturally enough say the Principle of Graciousness which has generated this relationship must in some fashion itself be involved in a similar relationship with us. Graciousness, in turn, seems only too eager to agree. In its most impressive theophanies it has repeatedly assured us that it loves us as a jealous lover.

We have been told by the Scriptures that God doesn't need our prayers. So we are forced to conclude that the main reason for praying is that we need to. We need to assert our unities with our fellowmen, with the world, and with the Graciousness of Being. We need to enter into dialogue with the Great Lover we suspect is out there. But there is a sense in which the Great Lover does need our affection. To the extent to which we are able to express that affection toward his Graciousness, we ourselves become more confident and more gracious. This enrichment of our personalities enables us to contribute more to the unfolding of the pilgrimage from the Alpha to the Omega. God's plan, in some dizzy, overwhelming twist, needs our co-operation. The more we pray, the better we are able to co-operate.

There is astonishing presumption in the notion that we insignificant earthlings can somehow or other demand the relationship of a spouse with the Graciousness of Being. Yet we do so, because there is something in our instincts that tells us that we may, and because the theophanies seem to have legitimated this instinct. But, like every other aspect of the good news, the lover relationship between us and the Graciousness of Being is really too good to be true, too marvelous to be taken seriously. If indeed we are loved, as was the faithless wife, or Mary Magdalene, or even the frightened spouse in *Belle de Jour*, then timidity, self-loathing, insecurity, anxiety are folly. The only appropriate response to this folly is laughter. If the Ultimate and Absolute loves us as a husband loves his beautiful bride, our fears are both childish and silly. In the face of the overwhelming evidence all around us we still persist in our diffidence, defensiveness, and self-loathing. The good news couldn't possibly be true. We would just be naïve and foolish if we permitted ourself to be taken in by it. Hopefully, the Lover can keep laughing at us.

But what is the Lover like? Man has asked himself this question ever since the idea of God began to be clarified in his mind. As some cynical anthropologist has put it, man has created God in his own image and likeness. This ought not to be very surprising, since the only tools we have available with which to think about God are the categories which our experience and culture have provided for us. So God has been described in terms appropriate for an Egyptian Pharaoh floating down the Nile River, a Semitic desert warrior, a pleasure-loving Homeric hero, a clever electrician, a proper English gentlemen, and a testy old Irish monsignor—to list but a few of the images of God which man has created after his own image and likeness. Such analogies are incomplete and inadequate and even deceptive, but can be purified and supplemented if we try to find signs of divinity in the world around us. He is like the love, the generosity, the patience, the kindness, the sensitivity, the delicacy, the beauty we see in other human beings. He is like the grandeur, the power, the harmony, the complexity of the material universe. He is like the energy, the recuperative powers, the nobility, the loyalty we occasionally glimpse, however dimly, in ourselves.

But, of course, the best image of God available to us is the theophany in Christ Jesus. One can see Jesus as a leader of a Jewish religious sect, as a rabbi learned in the law and skillful in the dialectical styles of the Jewish religion; one can even find great similarity between him and the leaders of the Essene communities by the shores of the Dead Sea, but I have always been astonished by those learned scholars that think that the Dead Sea Scrolls explain the uniqueness in the mystery of Jesus. The thing that is astonishing in a comparison between Jesus and the Essene is not the similarities but the differences; obviously, religious leaders appearing in the same time in history would have certain similarities; but the Essene "teacher of righteousness," however impressive he may be, does not belong in the same ball park with Jesus of Nazareth. The "teacher of righteousness" comes through as a stylized, abstract, and symbolic person with rabbinic wisdom that is beautiful indeed but neither flexible, nor imaginative, nor very powerful. Jesus, product as he was of his own time, towers above him. Even a completely secular reader of the New Testament is forced to admit that Jesus is scarcely limited by the time and space of which he was a part.

Some Scripture scholars insist that what we're seeing in the Scriptures is not so much a "live action" picture of Jesus, but rather, "an instant replay" fashioned by the early Christian community—a towering, dramatic, charismatic personality.

An even stronger case can be made for the vividness of Jesus of Nazareth if the picture is "an instant replay." If he looks that powerful, that attractive, that insightful, and yet that human in what is essentially an interpretation, what must he have been like firsthand? In the final analysis, the critical difference between Jesus of Nazareth and the "teacher of righteousness" is that the "teacher of righteousness" was forgotten for more than two millennia, until the caves of the Dead Sea were excavated, and Jesus of Nazareth was not forgotten and never will be. One man stayed buried and one man didn't. Jesus was a theophany manifesting God to man, showing man the things that were possible with God, he was also, to coin a Greek word which I suspect never existed, an "anthropophany," for in Jesus we have a clear demonstration of what man is capable of at his best.*

In a very real way, Jesus shows us the goal of our wanderings: the perfection of the human personality.† For Jesus was uniquely a man who accepted himself, who understood who he was and what he was about and how his energies were to be focused. While he was capable of fear, it was not a fear that dissuaded him from his goals. Timidity and excuses were completely foreign to him. He had an interpretative scheme, the will of his heavenly Father; he was able to give himself in love and to receive others' love in exchange without being threat-

* There is considerable resistance in certain Catholic circles to admitting that Jesus was a man. There is something in the rigid and reactionary manifestation of the Christian conscience that gets terribly upset by the assertion of Jesus' manhood and promptly retreats into a Docetist reaction. A parish in which I was once stationed was once condemned to the Holy Office by one of its members on the grounds that on Easter Sunday we preached strange and unusual doctrines about Jesus. Closer investigation revealed that the person's objection was to the reference in the scriptural account of the Resurrection where the angel says to the visitors to the tomb, "You seek the man Jesus. He is here no longer." Thus not only the priest who read the Testament, but the Scripture scholars who translated it, the Evangelist who wrote it, and presumably even the angel whose message was quoted were somehow or other guilty of preaching new and unusual doctrines about Jesus.

† I am not asserting here, let it be noted, that Jesus had a human personality in the sense that such a concept is rejected by traditional Catholic teaching. I simply mean that Jesus manifested the perfections of human nature, a human nature which in us is identified with the human personality.

The term personality means something different today than it did to the early Councils of the Church which defined Jesus as a person. I leave it to others more skilled at language, philosophy, and theology than I to demonstrate the relationship between these two meanings of personality and their implications in our talk about Jesus.

ened by it; he had great hope, the courage not to be intimidated by obstacles, the capacity to enjoy himself at parties (and even to keep them from being failures by working a miracle), discretion not to run risks needlessly until the appropriate time, precise care about rendering to others what was their due, an openness, an intimacy to both men and women, a respect for, and yet freedom from, the goods of this world, and finally, the ability to challenge and inspire others to the best of which they were capable. The model of the Christian life being presented in this volume was anticipated long ago by the man who wandered back and forth across Judea and Galilee, the man who was the mightiest theophany in history, the man who was God in a way that no other man could ever be, and the man to whom we can therefore address our prayers, because we realize that by addressing our prayers to him, we are speaking to God in the best manifestation that he has ever made.

The ultimate question which man must face, then, is whether he believes in the Graciousness of Being and Graciousness' love for us, or whether he does not. If he does, it is impossible for him to hold his tongue. He must respond, realizing that, while his response is confused, inadequate, and inaccurate, it is still his and is the best he can do. Either he responds and through his response seeks to initiate a union with Goodness that he hopes his wandering will enable him to make permanent; or he refuses to believe, refuses to respond, refuses to trust, and is faced with the awesome conclusion that his wandering is aimless.

Our wandering has purpose, to the extent that we maintain our successful dialogue with the Graciousness of Being. Our wandering assumes an ever stronger purpose and direction as we become more sensitive to Graciousness in ourselves, in others, in the material universe. We become, thus, more sensitive in our experimentation; our playing it by ear becomes more skillful; there is less time wasted, less detours are taken, less side paths investigated; we move with sure and steady instinct because we know where we're going and we have a clear idea of how we're going to get there. Wisdom consists essentially in a facility at dialogue with the situation in which we find ourselves. Prayer is the way that we find the way, the way we discover the meaning of self and of life; it is the unity which we now enjoy in anticipation and preparation for greater unity. It is hesitant, it is probing, it is difficult, it is uncertain, which is merely to say that it is part of wandering. Like the Indian brave who knows how to interpret the moss on the trees and can listen for sounds in the ground and can smell scent on the winds, the man who prays is able to read the signs of the times and, reading the signs of the times, he knows where to go.

12. *I Want to Buy a Commuter Ticket*

One hears in certain religious circles that it is no longer possible for an educated man to believe either in the resurrection of Christ or in his own personal resurrection. In a day of science, it is argued, the resurrection hypothesis is no longer tenable. With the rather astonishing glee that they reserve for "demythologizing" the central tenets of Christianity, some of our more au courant theologians are busily engaged in "demythologizing" the resurrection, that is, in explaining it in such a way that it is explained away. They are not terribly successful in making a resurrectionless Christianity more acceptable for their agnostic colleagues on university faculties, but presumably they do succeed in persuading themselves that it is possible simultaneously to be a Christian and not to be one.

The resurrection is, of course, at the core of Christianity. St. Paul left no doubt of it—"If Christ be not risen from the dead, then our faith is in vain." And St. Paul did not mean a metaphorical resurrection, a symbolical resurrection, a resurrection of a whole community, or an allegorical resurrection, Jürgen Moltman rather tartly observes that theologians who try to explain away the traditional interpretation of the resurrection do so at the risk of subscribing to a position that is at variance with

2000 years of Christian tradition. One supposes that there are many things that demythologizers can take away from Christianity that may improve it, and many other things that they can take away without seriously hurting it, but if they take away the resurrection, then Christianity does not remain.

There is something just a bit ironic in the unholy haste of some theologians to dismiss the resurrection as being untenable in an age of science, for the scientific positivism which they are so eager to appease is now much deader than the God they thought they had buried. God is not dead on the university campuses, save perhaps some of the divinity schools, but anyone who has taught concerned students realizes that scientific materialism is just about as dead as it can be.

Furthermore, the demythologizing theologians seem to think that it is only in our era that the resurrection has become a difficult doctrine. The Sadducees had a hard time believing it during the Lord's lifetime, and the Athenians put St. Paul to ridicule when he preached it. The resurrection has always been difficult to accept, but so, for that matter, has Christianity of which the resurrection doctrine is the core.

Either life or death is an illusion. The premise of the Christian wandering is that death is the illusion; yet we are not sure—and in the nature of things cannot be certain, not at least as we are certain of a mathematical theorem or of the laws of gravity, for the data are conflicting, the evidence not completely conclusive, and the arguments, no matter how frequently reworked, are not absolutely persuasive either way.

But it is still worthwhile, periodically, to attempt to present data for resurrection in different terms for the thought categories of a given age can bring new light to bear on the old issues. Perhaps the most brilliant reworking of the arguments for transcendence, and by implication, of the arguments for resurrection, in our time has not been done by theologians, but by my friend and colleague, Peter Berger in his superb book, *Rumors of Angels*. For Berger an angel is "a signal of the transcendent." That is to say, "a phenomenon that is to be found within the domain of our natural reality, but appears to point beyond that reality." Four of Berger's angels seem to me to be particularly persuasive. There is, first of all, the angel of trust. When a mother reassures a frightened child in the dark of night that everything is going to be "all right," she is, to Berger's mind, expressing a conviction about the nature of reality that is deeply rooted in man: "the very center of the process of becoming fully human . . . we find an experience of trust in the order of reality. Is this experience an illusion? Is the individual who represents it a liar?"

Berger's second angel is the angel of play. Little children are playing in the streets, standing in direct defiance of the threat of death. The joy of playfulness in some barely conceivable way implies the possibility of joy forever. "Joyful play appears to suspend, or bracket, the reality of our 'living towards death.'"

The third of Berger's angels is the angel of hope. Man has a strong urge to say "no" resolutely and even violently in the face of a threat to his existence. There is a tough, stubborn, unyielding part of our personality that simply refuses to concede that we can be wiped out. ". . . there is something in us that, however shamefacedly in an age of triumphant rationality, goes on saying 'no!' . . . In a world where man is surrounded by death on all sides, he continues to be a being who says 'no!' to death—and through this 'no!' is brought to faith in another world, . . ."

The fourth of Berger's angels is the angel of humor. Either laughter is an illusion or death is an illusion, for in the final analysis, one cannot really laugh if life is going to be snuffed out; and if death is an illusion, then the whole of life is a marvelous joke. "By laughing at the imprisonment of the human spirit, humor implies that this imprisonment is not final but will be overcome . . . (through) an intimation of redemption."

Berger's angels—trust, play, hope, and laughter—are not merely intimations of resurrection, intimations which no amount of cynicism can overturn, but also a hint of what resurrection would be like. The world of resurrection will be a world of trust, playfulness, hope, and laughter; it will be trust that will not be weakened by uncertainty, playfulness that need never come to an end, a hope of continuing fulfillment which cannot be frustrated or blighted, and laughter which finally understands the biggest joke of all.

We may not come to understand how these things can be, much less exactly what they will be like; and yet for those of us who believe in resurrection, trust, hope, playfulness, and laughter are ecstatic moments which give us some hint of what the future really will be like. There are many events in human life which combine trust, playfulness, hope, and laughter—the union between the sexes is one; the ending of a quarrel in which friendship makes a major leap to a new level of existence is another; a major breakthrough in our growth process, particularly when we share that growth process with someone else who has been counseling us, is yet a third. In all of these instances, if we hesitate between fearful and self-deceiving cynicism, on the one hand, and eager desire to believe and to live, on the other, something in us must die. The cowardly, lonely, neurotic, hesitant man in us must be put aside if the new man is to be put on. Whether it be in love making or expression of friendship or growth in personality—the act of dying is painful, the act of rising is glorious. Good Friday and Easter Sunday are inseparably linked.

Those of us who believe in the good news have a fair amount of empirical evidence running against our belief, but there are a number of phenomena with which those who do not believe in the good news are hard put to cope—trust, hope, play, and laughter. One can be a grim and serious atheist intellectual and write these all off as illusions, but even the atheist has somewhere within his being a signal of transcendence that still wants to say a violent "no!" to the idea that play, hope, trust, and laughter are an illusion. They seem to be too much part of the reality of man's life. They seem to be present at times when man is most fully himself and most fully human.

In the final analysis, one pays one's money and takes one's

choice; hope, trust, play, and laughter are either illusions and life is folly, or they are reality and despair is folly. Either commitment involves an act of faith, and in either we must choose which apparent reality is an illusion. Most of us Christians have some sort of intellectual commitment to the reality of the good news but are not quite able to live our lives as though we believe in the reality. Our humor, trust, hope, and playfulness are sadly deficient. Operationally, it may be very difficult to distinguish us from the most grim of the existentialist pessimists, save for the fact that we are often even less pleasant people than they. It is rather silly to believe in the good news and then not take advantage of it.

We can more easily believe the Rumors of Angels when we are young, but it gets more difficult as we grow older and find the physical life forces weakening and the reality of our death drawing much closer. Growing old is difficult at any time, but according to many critics, far more difficult in our society. In stable or slowly changing societies, the older man is the man who has had the most experience and hence is the wisest man and best able to interpret the meaning of reality for those around him. He is therefore respected and revered. But our world changes so rapidly that the wisdom and the experience of the old man is quite irrelevant to the young, who have a completely different set of problems and a completely different set of data to interpret. If a generation lasts but five years, as social scientists argue, a man who is approaching sixty is seven or eight generations away from the young radicals in their twenties. They can hardly expect him to know anything that would be at all useful or relevant to them.

The younger generation is unaware that "he who rejects history is condemned to repeat its mistakes." The young will cheerfully repeat the mistakes of the past on the pretext that they must first make their own mistakes. They will then be horrified when other young people persist in making the same mistakes again.

Thus growing old in a dynamic and changing society like ours is a double tragedy. One becomes not only physically weaker but technologically obsolescent. One has nothing to contribute either of strength or of wisdom to the important things that are going on in the world.

Yet Germany was led back from the ashes of the Second World War by a man who even in 1945 was called "the Old One," until recently France was presided over by a man who dominated its political life either by his presence or absence for almost thirty years, despite his somewhat sardonic comment that "I shall not fail some day to die." The General makes his predecessors, such as Bonaparte, Louis XIV, and Joan of Arc look like rank political amateurs. One suspects that if Dwight D. Eisenhower chose before his final illness to run for the Presidency of the United States, he could be elected again. Chairman Mao continues to preside over the new Chinese empire and Premier Salazar ruled for almost forty years. For Catholics, there is the splendid example of that funny old Italian gentleman who shook the Catholic Church to its roots as it has not been shaken since it left Jerusalem. Despite the attempts of his successor to eradicate the vital forces that Angelo Roncalli set in motion, no one seriously believes for a moment that the Johanine Revolution can be reversed.

So it is possible, even in such a dynamic and changing society as ours, for the old to have a great deal of influence. Who indeed was younger than Pope John? Is it then possible to stay young psychologically? The secret of accomplishing this, I suspect, is a certain fearlessness or personal security or even a stubbornness that does not ebb with bodily weakness. The secret of aging gracefully is to maintain an openness to options, or, in the terminology of this volume, to continue our wandering.

Most of us grow old in the fashion that we have lived. An optionless life, a secure and complacent and safe life leads to an optionless old age. We die long before our hearts stop beating but only because in our fear and in our timidity we deliberately chose to die. We grow old but we don't grow and we are dead long before we lie down. We are afraid of death because we have experienced it already. We do not believe, save timidly, in resurrection because we have experienced it constantly throughout life. Each new self-revelation after pain, each new attempt after failure, each new act of trust in response to others' love, each new experiment with our talents, each new change of viewpoint—all of these are resurrection experiences and each is another "signal of transcendence." If we permit ourself to experience resurrection as we live, then we have some inkling of what it will be like when we triumph over the final death.

But, what is resurrection like? Theologians assure us that it will be corporeal. Our body will be involved because we are bodily creatures and to the extent that we are separated from our bodies, our personalities are incomplete. Some theologians, such as Karl Rahner, suggest that the human personality needs an orientation toward matter in the state of temporary separation between personality and body which takes place at the time of death. The physical, human body that we now possess, presumably transformed in some marvelous fashion, is destined for resurrection; and this no Christian can deny.

Brian Wicker remarks that self-fulfillment continues more intensely after death; because the human personality has an infinite capacity for growth, there is no reason why growth cannot continue indefinitely. Thus the resurrection would include all the satisfaction we experience in personality growth.

The resurrection is also relational and will involve, presumably, a constant growth in our relationships. Sidney Callahan speculates that in the resurrection we can at last "return to the polymorphous perversity" of our childhood. She notes that the ultimate anguish of life as we know it is that we cannot be completely intimate with everyone, or, as she puts it, "We cannot have intercourse with everyone." In the resurrection experience, intimacy with everyone will be possible and there will be no barriers to the fulfillment of friendship. The question then arises as to whether there is sex in the resurrection experience. Many observers are inclined to say no, basing their reasoning on the Lord's comment that there is neither marriage nor giving in marriage in the resurrection. But, in the context in which the Lord made this statement, he was discussing marriage as a limitation on human relationships, trying as he was to explain to his disciples and the Sadducees how it was possible for a woman who had seven husbands to relate to all of them in the hereafter. He need only have been saying that the limitations that marriage imposes on human relationships do not exist in man's resurrected state.

Since the resurrection is corporeal, however, it does seem to follow that the post-resurrection relationships will also be corporeal. The resurrection will, in some fashion, necessarily be sexual, since man is sexual in every cell of his body. Exactly how this is going to work out in practice, of course, is scarcely something about which we have any information. The vision of unlimited sexuality which seems to be implied in our remarks might make the reader think that we anticipate some sort of Moslem heaven, an unlimited paradise of sexual delights. That the resurrection will be an unlimited paradise of sexual delights we do not doubt, though it will hardly be a Moslem heaven, both because the Moslem heaven seems to be essentially a male preserve and because sex in the Christian view of things is far more interpersonal than it could possibly be in the heaven of the Moslem warriors.

The combination of physical ecstasy and emotional satisfaction which results from intercourse between two people who are deeply in love is the best anticipation currently available to man of his permanent condition in the resurrected state. The powerful inspirational value of the sexual electricity and the awesome splendors of the human body will not be inhibited in the resurrection state as they are by the weaknesses of this world. The resurrection joys, then, will be interpersonal, physical, sexual, and corporate, because we enjoy them with others. They will be ecstatic, because the fears and the inhibitions and the insecurities and timidities which inhibit our ecstasy will have been stripped away.

But, unsatisfied with these delightful, but vague, speculations, man still wants to know what he will do in the resurrected state. The thought of floating on a cloud and strumming a harp indefinitely does not seem to be very appealing. Perhaps we should be effectively stopped by the Lord's remark that eyes have not seen nor ears heard nor has it entered into the heart of man those things which God has prepared for those who love him. Nevertheless, we're not quite prepared to give up that easily. It might be helpful to reread Marc Connelly's play *Green Pastures*. Assuredly the resurrection will not be a fish fry, though one would not on any a priori grounds want to exclude the possibility of fish fries being a part of it. One would misunderstand Connelly's genius to think, however, that he is asserting that paradise is a fish fry. What he is saying, rather, is that in the resurrection we will be engaged in activities much like those in which we engaged in our present life and yet very different from them. Professor Berger has given us some extremely helpful hints in his descriptions of the signals of transcendence, or, as he calls them, more poetically, the Rumors of Angels. Those experiences of our present condition which are the best tip-offs on our transcendent condition are such experiences as trust, hope, playfulness, and laughter. Theologians tell us that we need not have hope once we have obtained the goal of our wandering, and in the narrow technical definition of hope, I am sure they're right. But in the broader sense of the confident expectation of further growth and development, the resurrected life will surely involve hope. As for playfulness and laughter, Marc Connelly's fish fry is as good an anticipation as any.

In summary, then, resurrection is the ability to keep growing. We anticipate resurrection in our growth experiences in the present life and fulfill it in our growth experiences in the resurrected life. Salvation, therefore, is essentially loving enough to be able to give ourselves to others and in this repeated giving of self to others, continuing to grow. Damnation, on the other hand, is closing ourselves off from growth by closing ourselves off from others. Damnation is essentially a permanent state of loneliness, which Dante described very powerfully when he surrounded Satan by ice. The warmth of personal love, personal giving, and personal expanding is the way to salvation and the coldness of loneliness, fear, and turning in on the self is the way to icy damnation. We either give in trust and openness or we freeze to death.

There are many human persons who do not get the choice: those who die as children, or those who are physically or emotionally sick or ignorant, or so paralyzed with fear that for them decision is impossible. Sometimes one is inclined to suspect that perhaps the majority of men are, as the late French theologian Louis Billiot used to argue, moral infants, incapable of either salvation or damnation. We have no idea how many people are able to make the choice between openness and loneliness. We are forced to be satisfied with two propositions: (1.) Since God wills the salvation of all, he must, in some fashion that is unknown to us, compensate for the lack of freedom that afflicts so many human persons. (2.) The goal of human evolution is a situation where such divine compensations are either unnecessary or minimal. The goal of our corporate wandering is the creation of a society in which the maximum number of free human choices is possible. By such standards, it would appear that the wandering is going to go on for a long time.

Judgment is the determination of whether, in the context of our wandering, we have chosen for loneliness or for openness. We must continue to wander if we are to escape the negative judgment that, given the option of continuing on our wandering, or curtailing it, we chose to curtail it. Salvation comes through wandering. As we grow wiser and more sensitive, our journey becomes less obscure and uncertain. Our decisions must always, and necessarily, be short-run decisions, decisions that need to be re-examined critically to see if they are leading us toward the goal of our journey; but we become more practiced at making and reviewing decisions and simultaneously acquire a much better picture of what we are seeking. We know ourselves better—we know the world better; and through our dialogue we also know the Lover better. We are more conscious that not only is he out there, but he is also beside us as we travel on the road to Emmaus. So, as we approach the last things in life— death, judgment, resurrection—our confidence should increase. We should be like Pope John, more trusting, more secure, more playful; we know that Emmaus is near and that we will recognize the Lord there in the breaking of the bread.

Conclusion

The underlying theme of this book is one on which the writer can claim no monopoly: the spiritual life as it has been traditionally understood can be reconceptualized as a life of personal growth and development in the categories of contemporary behavioral science and of modern existentialist and personalist philosophy. The maturity and the self-fulfillment of the psychologist and the philosopher do not seem to mean anything too much different from what "perfection" meant to the writers of the traditional manuals. Both symbolize, however inadequately, the human goals of friendship, trust, and love. The traditional spiritual life lacked the flexibility and depth of insight that the social sciences provide, but the Christian would also argue that the social sciences lack in their turn the framework of ultimate values and goals that belief in the resurrection promise provides.

Our wandering is a search for the best that is in ourselves, the best which can only be discovered in a love relationship with others. So our quest is ultimately a quest for love, love for those with whom we are questing, love for the Absolute, which is the Object of our quest, and love for ourself, the subject of the questing. Our wandering is a love journey, one might almost say, a honeymoon.

Love makes demands: insistent, vigorous, and heavy demands. Because we love, there are demands that are made on us and because we love we must make demands on others. Yet we human beings seem singularly ill equipped both to make demands and to accept them. All our experience with demands in our formative years has led us to believe that demands are responsibilities which are preconditions for love. If others make demands on us, if they seem to impose responsibilities on us, it is because they expect us to prove our value and our love for them by living up to their demands. If we make demands on others, it seems that we're imposing on them responsibilities which are conditions that must be fulfilled before we are able to love them.

The most important insight of the spiritual life in the present time may well be that the most healthy and human of demands are not pre-conditions for love, but the result of it. Those who love us make demands on us not because they want to test our love but because they presume it. They see us at our best, they respect us as we really are, and they quite legitimately demand that we put aside our masks and our defenses and be ourselves. The responsibility is not one that they impose upon us from the outside, but rather, a responsibility that flows from that which we are. Our lovers are merely requesting that we be ourselves. What appear to be demands are, in fact, merely a reflection of that which is most truly us.

Similarly, when we make demands on others we ought not to stake the survival of our whole relationship on their response to our demands, but rather, do it in such a way that they realize without the slightest bit of doubt that we love them as they are, that we believe in them more than they believe in themselves, that we have more hope for them than they have for themselves, and that our love for them is far deeper than the love they are able to direct toward themselves. Our demands ought not to seek to impose greater responsibility, but rather, to liberate that which is the best in those whom we love, so that the warmth of our affection and our concern, trust, and friendship may enable them to flourish and grow.

Perhaps we need a new word instead of demands. The responsibilities that flow from deep and powerful human affection are really quite different from neurotic responsibilities, though the child in us is frequently unable to make the distinction; we can be poetic and name the demand the "call of the beloved"; we can be psychological and call it "trust toward fulfillment"; or we can be religious and call it "a journey to the heavenly kingdom." But whatever name we chose to use, the most serious obstacle to responding to the demands that flow from love or to imposing demands which are manifestations of love is our inability to believe the good news because it is too good to be true.

Life does matter. We are loved, we can grow and there is reason to hope. The sun does rise, the Omega point is out there and present in our midst. Lord help our unbelief!